98

PREDICTING THE FUTURE

PREDICTING THE FUTURE

From Jules Verne to Bill Gates

JOHN MALONE

M. EVANS AND COMPANY, INC.
New York

M. Evans and Company, Inc.
216 East 49th Street
New York, New York 10017

Library of Congress Cataloging-in-Publication Data

Malone, John Williams.
    Predicting the future : from Jules Verne to Bill Gates / John Malone.
        p. cm.
    Includes bibliographical references and index.
    ISBN 0-87131-830-X
    1. Forecasting—History. 2. Predictions—History. 3. Errors, Popular—History. I. Title.
    CB161.M35 1997
    003'.2—dc21   97-21360
                                                             CIP

Design and composition by John Reinhardt Book Design

Manufactured in the United States of America

First Edition

9   8   7   6   5   4   3   2   1

*This book is dedicated to
Vincent and Ellen McLaughlin,
who made it possible*

INTRODUCTION

Attempts to predict the future, to anticipate the unknown, are as old as humankind. The most ancient forms of prediction were religious in their import, prophecies of salvation or damnation and intimations of our spiritual fate, both in this life and in terms of some kind of afterlife. In the nineteenth century, with the start of the Industrial Age, a new kind of prediction came into being, as both scientists and writers of fiction began to imagine future technological innovations, extrapolating from what was already known. Scientists were primarily concerned with expanding human knowledge and gaining greater control over the world we live in, while fiction writers (and social visionaries) often focused on what affect new inventions would have on our everyday lives and the shape of society as a whole. The scientists were apostles of progress, but the writers were split into two camps, one envisioning the possibility of improving humankind and developing a more perfect world, while the other warned of the dire consequences of science run amok.

Arthur C. Clarke, who is both a scientist and a science-fiction writer, several of whose predictions are included in this book, has said that when an "expert" strays out of his or her own field to make a prediction, it is usually to state that something is impossible and the prediction is almost always wrong. You will find numerous examples here that validate his point. But it is also true that the experts can be astonishingly myopic even within their own area of expertise, which leads to truly embarrassing miscalls. We tend to be much harder on scientists who get it wrong than we do on imaginative writers who get carried away with their visions of the future. Jules Verne is celebrated for his many remarkable bull's-eyes and forgiven all the arrows that missed the target completely—after all, he was just telling a story. On the other hand, there is the great physicist Albert Michelson, who made the mistake of announcing in 1903 that all the fundamental physical laws had been discovered—just two years before Albert Einstein turned everything upside down. The fact that Michelson was subsequently awarded the Nobel Prize in Physics for work he had done earlier has not prevented physicists from laughing at his misguided certainty ever since.

Predicting the future is a perilous business. While a prediction that proves correct may considerably enhance your fame, your reputation can be forever clouded by a bad enough mistake. There are also those, several of whom you will meet in this book, who are best remembered for having got it dreadfully wrong—indeed, some poor souls are remembered *only* for that reason. The majority of the predictions in this book were made by scientists, but some of the most amazing were made by writers of fiction, who could of course indulge in reckless forecasts with greater impunity. Scientific and technological predictions are the book's central focus, but many other kinds of predictions are also included. You will find economic, political, and cultural predictions—most of them wrong, not only because the mistakes are more fun to read about, but also because nonscientific predictions tend to be more difficult to make and more often a matter of simple prejudice of one kind or another. And, of course, there are some predictions of the end of the world or of "civilization as we know it."

There are also some predictions in this book that focus not on future technological or social developments, but deal instead with the possibility of eventually proving theories about the past. That includes speculations about how the universe was formed and how it evolved; when astronomers peer beyond our own solar system they are in fact looking into the past, and the greater number of light years away another star system is, the further into the past they are gazing. Thus the prediction that black holes must exist could only be confirmed by future efforts to pinpoint them in the vast reaches of space where they were formed millions of years ago. But even on the Earth itself, answers to the mysteries of our own planetary history have often lain in the future—and many still do. Theories concerning such matters as the existence of a single huge land mass from which the known continents broke off, or that the extinction of the dinosaurs was the result of the impact of an enormous asteroid or comet, were initially met with skepticism. Yet in the years that followed, evidence was eventually uncovered to prove both theories correct. Although these theories concerned past events, their corroboration lay in the future, making them in that sense predictions that came true.

Given the nature of predicting the future, there are a lot of fancies in this book, but there are also a great many facts. Looking back over 140 years of predictions, we can see the history of the twentieth century unfolding, sometimes along expected lines but more often in ways that were wondrous, even jolting. What has happened since a young Jules Verne began predicting the shape of the twentieth century can give us at least some perspective on the twenty-first century that Bill Gates, and others like him, are now leading us into.

PREDICTING
THE FUTURE

1858 Impossibility of building the Suez Canal

Benjamin Disraeli

In 1858, The British Chancellor of the Exchequer, Benjamin Disraeli, rose in Parliament to attack the idea of British investment in the building of the Suez Canal. Disraeli was one of the greatest figures of nineteenth-century England, not only as a politician who would become Queen Victoria's favorite prime minister, but also as a successful novelist and intellectual leader. The construction of the Suez Canal was just getting under way in 1858, and Disraeli was echoing a widely-held view when he told Parliament that the effort was "a most futile attempt and totally impossible of being carried out." Part of his disdain, however, was no doubt due to the fact that the construction of the canal was being carried out by a company chartered by the French government. (A century later, many politicians would have the same reaction to the idea of constructing the "Chunnel" connecting France and England beneath the English Channel.)

The Suez Canal was to provide a direct route between the Mediterranean Sea and the Indian Ocean, thus making it unnecessary for ships to follow the lengthy route down the west coast of Africa, around the Cape of Good Hope, and north again along Africa's east coast. Given England's vast imperial holdings in India, the canal really should have been an English idea, but here were the French trying to pull it off. It should be said, however, that the construction of the one-hundred-mile waterway from Port Said on the Mediterranean to the Gulf of Suez,

1

despite making use of three lakes that lay along the route, was the most daunting engineering project yet undertaken in modern times. Many compared the effort to the building of the Egyptian pyramids two thousand years earlier, a feat that no one in the nineteenth century had really managed to explain, although it must have involved hundreds of thousands of slaves. Workers would actually be paid to build the Suez Canal, and the engineering problems hardly seemed less mind-boggling than the construction of the pyramids themselves.

In contrast to Disraeli's scorn, the building of the Suez Canal served as an inspiration to a young Frenchman by the name of Jules Verne. When the canal was begun, he was trying to make his mark as a playwright, without any great success. But then he turned to writing novels of adventure and speculation, achieving fame with his very first effort in this genre, *Five Weeks in a Balloon*, which was published in 1863. His second effort, *Paris in the Twentieth Century*, was turned down by his publisher as too fantastic. One of the elements of the story that bothered Pierre-Jules Hetzel, who also edited Balzac and Hugo, was that Verne had imagined twentieth-century Paris as a great port, the river Seine having been dredged to accommodate ocean-going vessels. If they could build a canal across the sands of Suez, Verne reasoned, why not bring ships to Paris!

The Suez Canal, ridiculed by Disraeli but a spark for Verne's imagination, was finally completed in 1869. The original canal was only 26 feet deep, with a bottom width of 72 feet and a surface width of 190 feet. But it would become a vital element in England's dominion over India during the next eighty years.

1863 ▸ Fax machines

Jules Verne

When editor Pierre-Jules Hetzel rejected Jules Verne's second novel, *Paris in the Twentieth Century*, he wrote, "No one today will believe your prophecy." The manuscript was found in 1989 in a safe thought to be empty, published in France in 1994 and in English translation, by Richard Howard, in 1996. It turned out to contain more astonishing predictions than any other work of Verne's. Horseless carriages run by gasoline engines based on Ferdinand Lenoir's 1859 invention, automated trains, electric lights making day of night—the forecasts are remarkable. And while Paris has not been transformed into the inland port Verne imagined, he also envisioned a five-hundred foot lighthouse standing at the head of the port, and placed it only yards from the exact spot where the Eiffel Tower was eventually erected.

Perhaps most astonishing of all, however, his Paris of 1960 had something we didn't get until a decade later: the fax machine. "Further," Verne writes, "photographic telegraphy, invented during the last century by Professor Giovanni Caselli of Florence, permitted transmission of the facsimile of any form of writing or illustration, whether manuscript or print, and letters of credit or contracts could now be signed at a distance of five thousand leagues."

How did Verne do it? By paying attention to everything that was going on around him in a world of explosive developments in technology, and then combining and extrapolating those inventions in new ways. The new technologies of photography and telegraphy already existed, so why not eventually pictures sent by wire? Today we have come to expect extraordinary technological developments to appear as a matter of course; we get annoyed when something like high-definition television takes longer to perfect than originally predicted. But in the nineteenth century, people were as often dazed as dazzled by the "newfangled gadgets" that kept popping up. The nervousness that many older people today feel about computer technology was evident across a much broader range of fields. From the mid-nineteenth to the mid-twentieth century there was always a tendency, even among experts, to cast doubt on the possibilities the future might hold. The atomic bomb, the landing on the moon, and the miniaturization of computer technology have knocked a good deal of the skepticism out of us. These days, the predictions that are most likely to get us to say, "Never in a million years," are sociological rather than technological. But in Verne's time, people were so busy trying to adjust to the changes that were taking place that they resisted many ideas about the future. Verne had no such problem, but the rejection of the manuscript of *Paris in the Twentieth Century* taught him a lesson. Instead of peering far into the future, he set his subsequent novels in a very recognizable nineteenth-century world. Rockets to the moon, yes, submarines, yes, but placed in the context of a world everyone already knew, where they could be accepted as fantasy rather than as visions of a coming reality.

1865 Manned travel to the moon, 1869 and back

Jules Verne

Jules Verne's *From the Earth to the Moon*, published in France as the American Civil War was drawing to a close in 1865, postulates a trip to the moon in the near future. It is led by one Impey Barbicane, president of the Gun Club, a society of artillery inventors supposedly founded in Baltimore, Maryland, to aid the Yankee cause against the Confederate states. Verne assumes a Union victory in the Civil War, which leaves the members of the Gun Club without a focus for the creation of their gigantic cannons. Barbicane thus proposes making a manned trip to the moon in a craft fired from a nine-hundred foot gun.

This was a wildly fantastic idea in 1865, but Verne was astonishingly correct in his predictions about a great many aspects of such a project, as the American space program would prove a century later. He foresaw the use of aluminum, because of its light weight, in building a moon vessel, although in his time the metal could be produced only by methods that were prohibitively expensive. The use of animals in the preliminary testing of the effects of weightlessness was employed in the novel, with Verne showing his sense of humor by having the test mouse devoured by the test cat in the course of the flight. The escape velocity calculated by Verne—12,000 yards per second—was correct, as was the flight time of 97 hours from the earth to the moon. The use of rockets to propel and steer the ship in space would become fact. Verne also placed his launch site on the Atlantic coast of Florida, only 134 miles from the eventual location of Cape Canaveral; moreover, his technical reasons for the choice of that location were the same ones NASA, which had originally wanted to blast off from Houston, eventually took into account.

Of course, the actual Apollo program used rockets for lift-off as well as for power in space. Yet by the 1990s, NASA had an equivalent of Verne's Space Gun on the drawing boards, with testing already under way, for use in the twenty-first century. Such a launching device, already nicknamed the "Verne Gun" by engineers, would cost a fraction of rocket blastoffs per flight. Thus Verne was in this regard even more prescient than it originally seemed when the first NASA flights began.

At the end of *From the Earth to the Moon*, the three intrepid explorers (Verne was also right about the number of crewmen), Impey Barbicane, Marcel Ardan, and Captain Nichols, are believed to have been trapped in an orbit around the moon. But Verne's sequel, *Round the Moon*, first serialized in 1869, brings the crew back to earth, with a splashdown in the Pacific Ocean. Here, Verne's foresight is almost uncanny. In 1969, after his voyage to the moon and back on Apollo 9, astronaut Frank Boorman wrote a letter to Verne's grandson, noting that his own capsule "splashed down in the Pacific a mere two and a half miles from the point mentioned in the novel."

1866 ▶ Maximum age of the sun 150 million years

Lord Kelvin

Lord Kelvin, born William Thompson, was one of the most respected and honored scientists of the nineteenth century. His scale of absolute temperatures, called the Kelvin scale, is a fundamental tool of science to this day. Using that scale, he subsequently calculated the age of the sun as 150 million years at most. This was a devastating blow to Charles Darwin, whose epochal *Origin of Species* was published in 1859. Darwin's theory of evolution depended on a time span of billions, not millions, of years to work. Fortunately for Darwin, other fields, particularly those of geology and paleontology, seemed to support his ideas, and pointed toward a time scale far grander than that suggested by Kelvin's calculations. What's more, Kelvin had added a parenthetical caveat to his findings: "I do not say there may not be laws which we have not discovered." Despite the ungainly triple negative in this sentence, it gave him a measure of protection that would prove invaluable nearly forty years later.

In 1901, Ernest Rutherford and Frederick Soddy discovered the nature of radioactive elements. These generate much more heat than their size would suggest was possible, some giving off heat for billions of years. This discovery not only validated Darwin, but showed that Lord Kelvin's estimation of the age of the sun was absurdly small. Imagine the horror, then, that Ernest Rutherford felt when he rose to deliver the first important paper on what he and Soddy had discovered in 1903. As Timothy

Ferris reports in *Coming of Age in the Milky Way*, Rutherford was appalled to see the now very elderly Lord Kelvin sitting at the back of the hall where Rutherford was speaking at the Royal Institution.

"To my relief," Rutherford wrote, "Kelvin fell fast asleep, but as I came to the important point, I saw the old boy sit up, open an eye and cast a baleful glance at me!"

At this point, the quick-witted Rutherford recalled Lord Kelvin's famous caveat. "Then a sudden inspiration came, and I said Lord Kelvin had limited the age of the earth, providing no new source (of energy) was discovered. That prophetic utterance refers to what we are now considering tonight, radium! Behold! the old boy beamed upon me!" Thus was a parenthetical hedge by one great scientist accorded the distinction of a splendid prediction by another, the second making a hedge of his own.

1868 ▶ Dreams of flying are fraudulent

London Daily Telegraph

The dream of men one day being able to fly went back to the ancient Greeks, but in the second half of the nineteenth century, making that dream a reality had become an obsession among many inventors. Such men were constantly carrying out experiments, announcing modest successes, and generally getting themselves into the newspapers on a regular basis. All this attention annoyed the editors of the *London Daily Telegraph* to the point that they announced their vexation in print: "Flying philosophers may be compared to . . . the proprietors of donkeys which are announced to ascend a ladder. The donkey never really goes up, and the philosopher has not yet flown."

Although the Wright brothers would not get off the ground for more than thirty years, the *Daily Telegraph* was ignoring a great deal of progress in the previous fifteen years. In 1853, Sir George Cayley, who laid the foundations for many principles of aerodynamics, built his third full-size glider—a tri-plane—put his coachman aboard as a passenger, and launched the plane on a trip from a hillside across a Yorkshire valley. The coachman had no controls—he was not a pilot in the true sense—but the result was still the first manned flight in history. On a smaller scale, another breakthrough was made in 1858 by a French naval officer named Felix Du Temple. He built a model airplane, designed a clockwork mechanism for it, and achieved the first successful flight of any kind using a powered device. In 1859 another crucial invention came when Ferdinand Lenoir designed the first gas engine. And in 1865, seventy years ahead of its time, Charles de Louvrier patented the first jet-airplane design.

Thus, even as the *Daily Telegraph* scoffed, many crucial elements of manned flight were already in place, waiting for future philosophers to get the donkey up the ladder.

1871 The element germanium

Dimitri Ivanovich Mendeleev

Novelists and utopian visionaries predict what humankind will create in the future. But scientists often make another kind of prediction: that something must exist even though it has never been observed. Such predictions are as often scoffed at as those of admitted fantasists, but the genius able to comprehend the existence of the yet undiscovered can also say, "Wait and see."

One of the great predictions of unseen reality was made by the creator of the periodic table of elements, Dimitri Mendeleev. When he began to compile his revolutionary table of the elements in 1869, giving each element an exact atomic weight, Mendeleev was faced with a serious problem. Although the elements could be neatly arranged in columns of seven that were linked as families by their physical properties on the horizontal lines, with their weights increasing vertically, he also had a number of gaps. Undeterred, he predicted what properties and weights these undiscovered elements would have. His most famous prediction concerned an element that he called "eka-silicon," with properties that lay between those of silicon and tin. It was twenty years before the element was indeed isolated in Germany, and was thus named germanium. Mendeleev had stated that the element would be 5.5 times heavier than water, that its oxide residue would be 4.7 times heavier than water, and listed a number of other chemical and other properties. All were found to be correct.

As Jacob Bronowski points out in *The Ascent of Man*, Mendeleev's ability to predict the nature of something that must exist but has not been observed is a perfect illustration of inductive reasoning, as opposed to deductive reasoning, which is based on what has already been discovered. Inductive reasoning follows from what is already known—in Mendeleev's case the elements that had been already isolated, weighed and defined—but requires an additional step to describe the as yet unknown. Human beings are much more comfortable with the known, the concrete, and even eminent scientists have often disputed, down through the ages, the inductive (often predictive) reasoning of those who dare to claim the existence of what has not yet been seen. Darwin, for instance, based his theory of evolution on what he had observed in terms of the divergence of development in particular species of birds and animals. That divergence had taken place was a matter of deduction; evolution, however, was an inductive theory that has its opponents in some quarters to this day. Mendeleev was making a smaller inductive leap in the case of germanium, and one whose accuracy he was fortunate enough to have confirmed in his own lifetime, but he had nevertheless described with absolute correctness something that was not at the time known to exist.

1872 ► Man will never fly with the power of his own muscle

H. Von Helinholtz

Although the gasoline engine had been invented in 1859 by Ferdinand Lenoir, most inventors working on aircraft in 1872 were still working with what were essentially gliders. A German skeptic of the time, H. Von Helinholtz, took note, writing, "It can scarcely be considered that man, even with the help of the most ingenious wing-like mechanism, depending upon his own muscular force, will be placed in a position to be able to raise his own weight into the air and to retain it there."

There were plenty of commentators around who said that human beings would never fly by any means except ascending in a balloon, who scoffed at the very idea of flight even with the aid of some kind of engine. But by limiting himself to scorn for the possibility of flying under sheer human muscle-power, Von Helinholtz carved out for himself a particularly honored place in the history of scientific skepticism. Machine-powered flight would arrive thirty years later with the Wright brothers, aerial bombing, solo flights across the Atlantic, transatlantic passenger service, helicopters, jet planes and rocket-powered flight—all routinely disparaged as impossible—would become reality, and still no one would have flown under the power of his or her own muscle. American astronauts would walk on the surface of the moon, again and again, and still Von Helinholtz's prediction would hold up. Maybe, after all, this was one kind of flight, imagined as far back as the ancient Greek myth of Icarus, that would never be realized.

But when it seems that something really can't be done, there are still stubborn individuals determined to show that it can. One such person was Paul MacCready, an aeronautical engineer with a doctorate from the California Institute of Technology. Not only did MacCready have a professional background in aeronautics, he was also a flying daredevil who had won the National Soaring Championship three times in sailplanes. In 1977, using new superlight materials, he constructed an aircraft called the *Gossamer Condor*. It was operated solely by pedal-power— like a bicycle with an ultra-sophisticated mechanism. Launched from a hillside, he pedaled blithely over a figure-eight course for a full mile above California's San Joaquin Valley. One hundred and five years after the fact, Von Helinholtz's negative prediction finally bit the dust. Two years later, pedaling a new aircraft called the *Gossamer Albatross*, MacCready must have given any ancient mariners out in small boats a serious scare as he flew across the English Channel using the power of his own legs.

1876 ▶ The telephone: A toy no one would want to use

Gardiner Green Hubbard,
President Rutherford B. Hayes

The patents filed by Alexander Graham Bell for the telephone proved to be the most valuable in United States history. But while he knew exactly what he had, a lot of very important people dismissed his invention in quite contemptuous terms. Bell did not create the telephone out of whole cloth; others had been laying much of the technical foundation for years. But Bell had intimate knowledge of a crucial element that others lacked. He, like his father, was trained as an elocutionist, and used this background to develop pioneering techniques for teaching the deaf to speak. Beginning in 1872, he had his own school for the deaf in Boston, Massachusetts. What he knew about the human voice made it possible for him to achieve a technical breakthrough in 1876 that resulted in the famous first transmission between himself and his assistant, Thomas Watson.

Everyone saw that what he had achieved was wondrous, and his fame was immediate. But there was great skepticism about its usefulness. His prospective father-in-law, Boston lawyer and one of the founders of the National Geographic Society, Gardiner Green Hubbard, patted Bell on the back and announced in the dismissive tone so often heard by sons-in-law-to-be, "It's only a toy." Bell knew better, and was busy arranging demonstrations for investors and politicians. But at one of these he was put down by none other than President Rutherford B. Hayes, who said, "That's an amazing invention, but who would ever want to use one of them?"

Hayes, the only President to win fewer popular votes than his opponent, but gaining office through the vagaries of the electoral college, failed to win reelection. Bell married Mabel Hubbard in 1877, became an immensely rich man, and succeeded his father-in-law as president of the National Geographic Society in 1898.

1880 No commercial value to phonograph

Thomas Alva Edison

Thomas Edison was the greatest of American inventors, to the degree that a recent biography by Neil Baldwin is subtitled "Inventing the Century." Of all his extraordinary creations there was none about which he cared more, or that gave him more trouble, than the phonograph. The first quite crude machine, which recorded sound on tinfoil wrapped around a cylinder, was demonstrated at his Menlo Park, New Jersey, laboratory and then for the editors of *Scientific American* in New York City at the beginning of December, 1877. It caused a sensation; the famed spiritualist Madame Blavatsky soon acquired one, and Alfred, Lord Tennyson heard his own verses played back at the first demonstration in London. Yet in fact the machine didn't work terribly well, requiring considerable manual dexterity and a thorough understanding of its quirks. Edison was soon caught up in a much more lucrative enterprise, the opening of his first electric power plant, and he put the improvement of the phonograph aside. By

1880, he had become so downhearted about the future prospects of the recording device that he told his assistant Sam Insull, "The phonograph is not of any commercial value."

As late as 1886, when his close friend and sometime business partner Ezra Galliland tried to steer him back to work on the phonograph, Edison put him off. As Neil Baldwin relates in *Edison*, "Edison countered in exasperation that his initial patents had expired, the concept would never grow beyond the novelty stage in the minds of consumers, the Edison Speaking Phonograph Company existed on paper only, and besides, the field was wide open; the Volta Laboratory Association run by Alexander Graham Bell had in fact built several 'graphophones' during Edison's downtime." Eventually, Edison did return to the problem, but he had great difficulty in finding the formula for his new wax recording cylinder, and it was not until the turn of the century that the new machines went into large-scale production.

By 1907, the new Victor Talking Machine Company and the Columbia Company were presenting a new recording format using disks instead of cylinders. Edison was initially reluctant to move in this direction, but his machines began to fall sharply in sales, and he gradually developed an improved disk machine of his own, with a diamond stylus playing on a vinyl-coated disk. The final effort produced such remarkably good sound that halls were rented around the country where a live singer would perform with a Diamond Disc machine, the lights lowered at intervals during which audience members were asked to guess whether the singer or the disk was being heard. At last, Edison had the full-fledged commercial success he had disparaged 35 years earlier.

Although Edison's doubts about the commercial value of the phonograph make for a good story, it is not all that unusual for an inventor to be unsure about the value of his or her own creations. When the great British inventor Michael Faraday built the first dynamos in the 1830s, a skeptical Sir Robert Peel asked him of what use the machine was. Faraday replied that he wasn't sure yet, but then added, "I wager that one day your government will tax it." Forty years later, of course, dynamos were used to create the power for Thomas Edison's first electric plant. And as soon as electric lighting began to spread across the country, states began taxing power plants. The phonograph and the records played on it also eventually became taxable items, a sure sign of commercial success.

1883 ▶ Astronomical advertising

Villiers de l'Isle-Adam

"Astronomical advertising" does not refer to the cost of a thirty-second commercial on the Super Bowl broadcast, but rather to the physical projection onto the heavens of advertising logos and copy. This idea was first suggested by the French writer Villiers de l'Isle-Adam, in a short story called "Celestial Publicity" that appeared in his collected *Cruel Tales* in 1888. L'Isle-Adam, following in the popular footsteps of Jules Verne, wrote a number of future-oriented stories and novels, although his approach was both more literary and more mordant than Verne's, closer to the Edgar Allan Poe example. His work is still occasionally included in anthologies of fantasy stories, and in his time he was very widely read. In "Celestial Publicity," he imagines an advertisement projected on the constellation Ursa Major. "Would not the Great Bear herself have cause for astonishment," he writes, "if, between her paws there suddenly appeared this disquieting question: 'Are corsets necessary?'" (The translation was made in 1963 by Robert Baldick.)

The technology for pulling off such a stunt did not exist in de l'Isle-Adam's time, but even back then the precursors of today's Madison Avenue admen were known for their wild ideas about how to attract the public's attention. Today, laser technology would make it entirely feasible to project an advertisement on the face of the moon. To prevent the Man in the Moon from suffering the kind of indignity de l'Isle-Adam imagined for Ursa Major, a ban on using the face of the moon in such a way was included in the international space treaty signed in 1989. Villiers de l'Isle-Adam was way ahead of his time and right on the mark.

1888 ▸ The credit card

Edward Bellamy

Edward Bellamy's *Looking Backward* was one of the most popular American novels published in the last twenty years of the nineteenth century. Unlike most best-sellers, it is still read today, due to its charm and genuine breadth of imagination. The novel is set in the Boston of the year 2000, where society has evolved into a socialist utopia. Although money as such has been abolished, it is necessary to have an old-fashioned equivalent to spend on the less up-to-date continent of Europe. (The idea that Europe was behind the times had much to do with the novel's popularity in America.) Bellamy thus conceived of having American travelers in Europe carry credit cards, which he noted were "just as good in Europe as American gold used to be."

When individual American banks actually began to issue credit cards to their customers in the 1950s, they did not of course consult Bellamy's novel for the name they gave to this new product. It was simply that Bellamy had come up with the obviously apt term for them more than sixty years earlier. The real growth of credit cards came in the late 1960s, with the introduction of the BankAmericard and Master Charge. By 1973, even second-tier restaurants, hotels, and shops in Europe had American bank credit card logos plastered in their windows, but some were still reluctant to honor them. There was good reason for this, as Americans making a charge to a credit card in say, Florence, Italy, subsequently discovered: it could take as many as three to four months for the charge to appear on their credit card bills. This happy circumstance did not last long, of course. By the late 1970s, improved computer technology saw to it that a charge made in Europe showed up on one's bill just as quickly as a purchase at the local mall at home. But that meant that credit cards, not just in Europe but around the world, had indeed become, just as Bellamy had predicted, "as good as American gold used to be."

1891 ▸ Aluminum the metal of the future

Charles Martin Hall

Aluminum is the most abundant metallic element in the crust of our planet, and in one form or another is also present in almost all plants and animals. But it never appears in metallic form in nature. It was first identified by Sir Humphrey Davy in 1809, and given the name aluminum, but what he produced was only an iron-aluminum alloy. The metal was isolated by Hans Christian Ørsted in 1825, and the next step was taken by the German chemist Friedrich Wohler two years later, when he managed to produce an aluminum powder. In 1845, Wohler succeeded in creating actual globules of metal; its sheen created something of a sensation when it was shown at the Paris Exposition of 1855, but the method of producing it was so expensive and so tedious that it remained little more than a curiosity for another thirty years. An American chemist named Frank F. Jewett studied with Wohler in Germany and went on to become a professor of chemistry at Ohio's Oberlin College. As Royston M. Roberts relates in *Serendipity*, "In the 1880s Jewett often called the attention of his students to the unfortunate fact that although aluminum was the most abundant metal, no one had been able to extract it from its complex ore by a practical process." A day student at the college, Charles Martin Hall, became fascinated with this problem, and set about trying to produce aluminum by electrolysis—a process then becoming common thanks to Thomas Edison. By melting the mineral cryolite and adding to it the common aluminum ore bauxite, and then passing an electric current through the mixture, he produced shiny pellets of the metal. Acting on Jewett's advice, he immediately applied for a patent—and none too soon. He had produced his result on February 23, 1886; within a month, the French chemist Paul-Louis-Toussant Heroult independently arrived at the same solution. With his prevailing patent in hand, Hall and a group of young businessmen founded the Aluminum Company of America (ALCOA), originally called the Pittsburgh Reduction Company, and began manufacturing tea-kettles, aluminum sheets, and the raw metal. Hall and his cohorts claimed it was the metal of the future. It did have enough immediate uses, particularly in the kitchen, so that the company was able to obtain its first bauxite mining rights by 1899. But the real future of aluminum still lay ahead, awaiting the invention of the airplane. It really came into its own as larger airplanes began to be built in the 1920s; the light weight of the metal alone made it ideal for aircraft construction. The Earth's most abundant metal thus became the casing for the planes that flew far above its surface.

1892 ▸ Munitions as an end to war

Alfred Nobel

The inventor of dynamite and munitions tycoon Alfred Nobel was extremely sensitive to charges that his wealth was founded upon the ingredients of mass destruction, and that he ruled an "empire of death." He established the Nobel Peace Prize and the literary and scientific awards that bear his name in an attempt to prove that he was, at heart, a friend to the human race. This was not just a matter of public relations to Nobel. Many later philanthropists, from John D. Rockefeller to Andrew Carnegie, saw charitable trusts quite plainly as a way to redeem the family name, and to undermine charges of ruthlessness and exploitation. But Alfred Nobel was a more complicated case.

In 1892, for example, he had told a pacifist organizer, "My factories may make an end to war sooner than your congresses." He believed that armaments, equally distributed among great powers, would threaten a carnage so vast that mere common sense would lead countries to forge a lasting peace rather than engage in mutual destruction. The First World War, of course, proved him to be utterly wrong in this supposition, becoming the bloodiest conflict in human history—even more appalling, in terms of battlefield casualties, than the Second World War would prove to be, although the second upheaval would have much greater civilian casualties because of aerial bombing and the Holocaust. But although he was wrong about the munitions he manufactured, the development of nuclear bombs did ultimately create, during the Cold War era from 1946 to 1993, a half century "balance of terror," as it came to be known, that forestalled world war even as conventional weapons continued to be used in Korea, Vietnam, the Middle East, and other smaller conflagrations. The concept of "mutually assured destruction" as a recipe for an uneasy peace, despite such frightening moments as the Cuban missile crisis of 1962, became operative when the weapons of war became sufficiently powerful. Along the way, almost all the physicists whose work led to the creation of nuclear weapons received a Nobel Prize.

1895 Intelligent life on Mars

Percival Lowell

Every fifteen years, Mars swings particularly close to the Earth as it orbits the sun, approaching within 35 million miles (in other years, its closest approach may be as far away as 65 million miles). During the close approach of 1877, Mars was studied in detail by the Italian astronomer Giovanni Schiaparelli, who claimed to see numerous long, straight lines on the planet. He called these lines *canali*, a word which he meant as "channels," but which, according to common practice, was translated into English as "canals." Canals implied that something had been built, and that in turn implied to some people that intelligent beings must have done the building. Schiaparelli did not rule out such a possibility, but he initially emphasized a natural explanation, noting the existence on Earth of such geological features as the English Channel. While most other astronomers failed to even see the canals or channels Schiaparelli had observed, a few backed him up, most notably the French astronomer Camille Flammarion. Flammarion had many serious credentials, but was also given to sensationalistic speculations (see his doomsday prediction for 1910).

The astronomer who took the idea of Martian canals most seriously, however, was Percival Lowell of the famous Boston family. Lowell had the financial resources to build his own observatory, in conjunction with Harvard University, in Flagstaff, Arizona. Although he would subsequently make some important contributions to astronomy, including calculations that eventually led to the discovery of the planet Pluto in 1930, Lowell got carried away in his observations of Mars. The Flagstaff observatory opened just in time to study Mars during its close approach in 1894, and Lowell saw just what he was looking for—a classic case of bad science proceeding from preconceived ideas. Lowell mapped a total of 184 canals, more than double the number previously observed by Schiaparelli. Lowell had answers to every objection about his findings. For example, the lines he claimed to see would have to be at least thirty miles wide to be apparent through his telescope, but Lowell explained that away by positing lush vegetation growing on either side of the canals themselves. Although he did note in his 1895 book *Mars* that other explanations were possible, he insisted that his evidence strongly backed up the existence of intelligent life on the red planet. He did have the good sense, however, to refuse to speculate on what those beings might look like.

Despite Lowell's proselytizing, most astronomers remained extremely dubious; indeed, many of the most eminent could not even make out the lines Lowell claimed to see. But the popular press had a field day with the idea, and H. G. Wells's, famous 1898 novel, *The War of the Worlds*, was directly inspired by Lowell's work. At the turn of the century, a Paris newspaper went so far as to offer a 100,000 franc reward to the first person who could prove that he or she had encountered intelligent life from another planet—but Martians wouldn't count because it would be too easy to meet them! Lowell's influence was also behind the eleven Edgar Rice Burroughs novels about Mars, the first of which was published in 1911; in their time, these books were even more popular than his Tarzan novels.

Unfortunately (or fortunately, if one goes by the H. G. Wells concept of Martian life), it turned out that Lowell's canals were no more than an optical illusion brought on by wish-fulfillment. It is possible that microbial life forms have existed on Mars, as suggested by the discovery of the apparent "Mars Rock" of 1996. But all the evidence produced by today's high-powered telescopes, as well as that collected by the unmanned Viking probes that landed on the Martian surface, speaks against the idea that there was ever intelligent life on Mars, let alone a sophisticated Martian civilization. Many of today's scientists find that as disappointing as Percival Lowell would have.

1895 "You will never amount to anything"

Einstein's Greek teacher

At the age of sixteen, Albert Einstein was attending school at the Luitpold Gymnasium in Munich. He was a lively, fun-loving boy who did not seem to be much interested in his studies. His Greek teacher, fed up with young Albert's lack of focus and application, made one of those predictions of failure that appear ludicrous in retrospect when applied to people who turn out to be enormously talented and famous, and yet are probably quite true when said to most other students. Einstein did not in fact shine as a student, either at school or at college, and was employed in the lowly position of patent clerk when at the age of twenty-five he began writing the four papers that would forever change the nature of physics and the way in which we view the universe. But the intense curiosity and speculative habits of mind that were characteristic of his genius had actually begun when he was very young. It was just that as a teenager and young man nothing he was being taught was sufficiently challenging to provoke his real interest.

What's more, Einstein was in good company. If he was the most revolutionary thinker of the twentieth century, along with Freud, the most revolutionary thinker of the nineteenth century was certainly Charles Darwin. And when he was fifteen, his own eminent father said to him, "You care for nothing but shooting, dogs, and rat-catching, and you will be a disgrace to yourself and all your family." Once again, Darwin's love of wandering about the countryside, his fascination with nature, and particularly his rat-catching were early signs of the particular direction in which his genius would lead him. For him, everything finally came into focus during his four-year around-the-world voyage as recording naturalist aboard H.M.S. *Beagle*, another rather lowly position and one for which the ship's captain thought he might not be well-enough equipped.

It should hardly be surprising that men like Darwin and Einstein are initially underestimated. Society has always been organized to reward those who are best at taking advantage of the status quo, although they are not the ones who move the world forward. A notable study was carried out by William Bender, the dean of admissions for Harvard College in the 1950s, which revealed that the Harvard graduates who went on to do the most creative work were seldom those who graduated at the top of their classes. The students who got the best grades almost always became successful, and sometimes made a lot of money, but the ones who made the breakthroughs in the arts and in science were often in the second or even third tier in terms of grades. Why? Because they were too busy thinking about other things than their required courses—just as Einstein and Darwin were.

1899 ▶ Everything has now been invented

Charles H. Duell

In 1899, Charles H. Duell, the commissioner of the U.S. Office of Patents, wrote to President McKinley, urging him to abolish the patent office. "Everything that can be invented has been invented," he said.

The original U.S. patent office had been voted into existence in 1790. It was run by the secretaries of state and war, and the attorney general. The secretary of state was Thomas Jefferson, an inventor of note himself, although he never patented any of his own creations, publishing their specifications instead, so that anyone could make use of them and no could take them over to make money from. The law was revised and liberalized in 1793, taking the onus of acting as patent clerks off the shoulders of cabinet ministers. In 1836, after a fire destroyed most existing records, a new patent act was passed that established an independent agency, headed by a commissioner of patents.

It was in this position that Duell proclaimed an end to invention. Perhaps this was in part due to the usual fin de siècle fever, which has always led to such pronouncements (in the 1990s we have had serious books announcing the end of history and the end of economics, among other things). Or perhaps Duell had simply had his mind boggled by the number of wonders created at the end of the nineteenth century. Patents had already been issued for electric lights, the telephone, the automobile, and moving pictures, not to mention the zipper. Duell was, of course, somewhat premature. During the next decade, new inventions abounded, with patents being issued for everything from the Wright brothers' "flying machine" to Gillette's safety razor. Since the first patent law went into effect in 1790, well over five million U.S. patents have been granted, and that's not even counting unpatented creations such as chemical substances, which have been accumulating over the past four decades at the rate of several hundred thousand per year.

It is true that a hundred years after Duell's pronouncement the number of purely mechanical inventions is slowing down, despite the fact that in a number of areas "the better mousetrap" has yet to be devised. The future of invention appears to be tilting toward the microscopic, in fields like chemistry, biology and computer technology. But no one is now suggesting that the Patent Office should go out of business. We have instead come to expect a steady diet of new wonders, to believe that the unimaginable is just around the corner, down the road to infinity.

1900 ▸ An end to war in the twentieth century

Andrew Carnegie

In 1900, Andrew Carnegie wrote an optimistic essay on the achievements that could be looked forward to in the century that had just begun. The great steel magnate and philanthropist quite naturally saw a continuing development of the industrial wonders that had transformed the world in the second half of the nineteenth century, and from which he had amassed billions that he then turned around and gave away in a largely successful effort to obscure his reputation for ruthlessness in business. In this vein, he also persuaded himself that industrial and technological advancement would serve to improve the overall human condition and outlook. Thus, he predicted, there would be an end to war in the coming century: "To kill a man will be as disgusting as we in this day consider it disgusting to eat one," he wrote, using oddly rapacious language to convey his idea of peace.

Unfortunately, the twentieth century proved to be the bloodiest in this history of the world. World War I, with its introduction of trench warfare, the machine gun, and tanks (many of them made of Carnegie steel), brought a level of carnage never before imagined, almost wiping out a generation of young men in Europe. World War II brought not only the horrors of the Holocaust, with six million Jews put to death as part of Hitler's "final solution," but a total death toll of at least fifty million human beings around the world. "Small" wars in Korea and Vietnam, civil wars in Bosnia and many African countries, brutal ethnic conflicts in the Middle East, and astounding death tolls from gang wars, criminal activity, and domestic violence in gun-happy America, all helped to make a mockery of Carnegie's vision of the future. But as the "bloodiest century" draws to a close, at least there are few voices offering up the kinds of false hope that Carnegie and many others indulged in one hundred years ago.

1902 Submarines as death traps

H. G. Wells

In 1902, the world famous author of *The Invisible Man* and *The War of the Worlds*, H. G. Wells, wrote, "My imagination refuses to see any sort of submarine doing anything but suffocate its crew and founder at sea." This was a surprising statement, both in terms of the date it was made and by whom it was made.

The first practical submarine, after all, had been designed and built during the Revolutionary War by a Yale undergraduate named David Bushnell. His vessel, called the *Turtle*, was launched in 1776 and proved capable of staying underwater for a full half hour. It introduced such concepts as the screw propeller and underwater ballast tanks for submarines. The explosive mines it carried were meant to be attached below the water line to enemy vessels, timed to explode after the submarine had made its getaway. An unsuccessful attempt to do just this was carried out in 1776 against the flagship of Lord Admiral Richard Howe, which was anchored in Boston Harbor. The failure did not involve a malfunctioning of the submarine, but rather that the single crew member aboard the Turtle met unexpected difficulty in attaching the mine. After the war, George Washington said, "I then thought and still think the *Turtle* was an effort of genius."

The great steamship inventor, Robert Fulton, took the submarine several steps further in 1800, building a four-man prototype for the French, which was able to remain submerged for an hour. Napoleon refused to provide funds for larger versions, however, apparently because French naval officers regarded the whole idea of underwater

weapons as unworthy of national military valor. Fulton
built a larger submarine, the *Mute*, for use against the
British in the War of 1812. Powered by a steam engine
when running on the surface, and twin propellers, it was
eighty feet long and could proceed at four knots an hour
underwater. It towed mines behind it, which were used
to blow up a 200-ton vessel in a test run. But a sudden
gale came up during a planned attack on the British fleet
in Long Island Sound in 1814, and the *Mute* ran around,
and was subsequently destroyed by the British.

Other experimental submarines were built over the next
several decades, but the next to be used in war was the
Confederate submarine *H. L. Hunley*, which became the
first to sink an enemy ship on February 17, 1864, when it
attacked the 1,240-ton Union blockader U.S.S.
Housatonic, off Charleston, South Carolina. But, as detailed in Volume 2 of *U.S. Submarines* by Henry C. Keatts
and George C. Farr, the career of this vessel was marred
by tragedy; it sank four times, and a total of thirty-two
sailors lost their lives aboard it. After the Civil War, a submarine designed of O. S. Halstead and called the *Intelligent Whale* was built for the U.S. Navy and had a
successful first test, but three subsequent crews totaling
thirty-nine men were killed.

The histories of the *H.L. Hunley* and the *Intelligent
Whale* may well have fueled H. G. Wells's doubts about
submarines, but there were considerable successes to follow in the years before he made his statement. Simon
Lake's *Argonaut* of 1897 was the first to make long runs
in the open sea, eventually amassing 2,000 miles of such
voyages. It was a front page sensation around the world,
and brought Lake a letter of congratulations from Jules
Verne. An Irish immigrant to the United States, John P.
Holland, began building submarines in 1875. He finally
came up with a vessel that passed trials witnessed by

Admiral George Dewey in March 1900. Propelled by a gasoline engine while on the surface and an electric motor when submerged, it had a conning tower and tanks for reserve fresh air, and was capable of covering 1,500 miles at sea. Its design, dubbed Class A, soon became the international standard.

With the success of the *Holland*, 125 years of experimentation, much of it also successful in more limited terms, had resulted in the launching of a new age of naval endeavor. Why then, at this very late date, was H. G. Wells so damning, and so wrong, in his comment on submarines? He was a futurist himself, after all, and his refusal to see the potential of the submarine seems almost irrational. Perhaps, in fact, it was just that. The most famous of all submarines, the undersea home and laboratory of Captain Nemo, called the *Nautilus* in tribute to Robert Fulton, had brought Jules Verne worldwide acclaim when *Twenty Thousand Leagues Under the Sea* was published in 1870. And Wells detested Verne's novels. He believed his own books to be vastly superior both in intellectual content and in style—although, in fact Verne's work was better grounded in science. To make matters worse, Wells was constantly being compared to Verne by critics. Thus it seems likely that Wells's bias against submarines stemmed from his dislike of Jules Verne.

1902 ▸ No special highways for automobiles

Harper's Weekly

By 1902, only about four in every 10,000 families owned an automobile, but that was enough to keep the early carmakers busy and profitable. Ransom E. Olds had just introduced the first experimental production line, and the manufacture of most cars was a time-consuming process. Even so, many people realized that the automobile was eventually going to eclipse the horse and buggy altogether, and there began to be a great deal of talk about building paved roads just for cars. This caused the editors of one of the period's preeminent magazines, *Harper's Weekly*, to comment, "The actual building of roads devoted to motor cars is not for the near future, in spite of many rumors to that effect." This is sometimes listed as a foolish prediction, but in some ways it was quite accurate.

It is true that the larger cities quite quickly began paving their roads with that hard surface named for its Scottish inventor, John McAdam, and because automobiles made people venture farther afield, new roads were constructed in many places. But the kind of express highway now clogged with automobiles from one end of the country to the other was quite slow in coming. The first true expressway was New York's Bronx River Parkway, which wasn't completed until 1925, almost twenty years after it was first conceived. Similar highways were constructed around cities in the remaining years before World War II, but many major highways were simply old roads that had been broadened. By the time Dwight D. Eisenhower became President in 1953, the lack of superhighways across the most advanced country on earth was becoming something of a national embarrassment. Because it had to rebuild the entire nation, our World War II enemy, Germany, was in the process of building its famous *autobahns*, making interstate travel in America look backward by contrast. Eisenhower thus proposed a massive federal program of which Democrats rather than Republicans are supposed to be so fond. With bipartisan support, since it was worked out to include largess for every state, the Interstate Highway Act of 1956 was passed. It provided $33.5 billion to construct 42,000 miles of interstate highways across the nation.

Thus, nearly sixty years after the skeptical *Harper's Weekly* editorial comment, a national system of "roads devoted to motor cars" finally began to be constructed. That system boosted the sale of cars and the consumption of gasoline, made a household name of Holiday Inn—a company started only in 1954—and steadily increased the number of tourists at National Parks to the point that some of them are now virtually overrun. Future historians will decide what special moniker to give the twentieth century, but the Interstate Highway System made "The Age of the Automobile" a plausible candidate—one that *Harper's Weekly* clearly did not have in mind in 1902.

1903 No more physical laws
1928 to be discovered

Albert Michelson, Max Born

In 1903, the American physicist Albert Michelson said, "The more important fundamental laws and facts of physical science have all been discovered, and these are now so firmly established that the possibility of their ever being supplemented is exceedingly remote." This was an odd statement to come from someone who had himself upset the scientific applecart sixteen years earlier. In 1887, Michelson, working together with Edward Morley, had shown that there could be no *aether*, the invisible cosmic wind on which light was supposed to travel. In one aspect or another, this idea had been around for centuries. But the Michelson-Morley experiments had shown that variations in the velocity of light that should occur if there was an aether did not in fact exist. Ironically, this very finding played a major part in causing Einstein to look in new directions. Even as Michelson was saying that new discoveries in physics were remote, Einstein was beginning to formulate his revolutionary Special Theory of Relativity, which he would publish two years later, in 1905.

Michelson's premature announcement should have served as a warning to other physicists, but twenty-five years later, in 1928, Max Born, one of Einstein's most important followers, announced, "Physics as we know it will be over in six months." He was moved to make this statement by Paul Dirac's success in working out the equations governing electrons. All that seemed to remain to do was to work out the equations for protons. But three years later, Leo Szilard came up with the idea, while standing on a London street corner, of the chain reaction as the key to unlocking the energy of the atom.

Michelson and Born were both great scientists; the former was awarded the Nobel Prize in Physics for 1907, and the latter received it in 1954. But their genius did not protect them from the temptation to believe that all mysteries had been revealed. In his best-selling book, *A Brief History of Time*, Stephen Hawking brings up Max Born's statement as a cautionary note, but even Hawking has recently been saying that a "unified theory" of physics may be just around the corner. A unified theory that manages to tie together the bizarre world of quantum physics and the concrete world of Newton's gravitational laws is the holy grail of contemporary physics. To find it would mean that everything had been explained. Don't bet on it.

1904 ▸ World-wide communications

Nikola Tesla

Born in 1856 into a well-to-do Serbian family, Nikola Tesla emigrated to the United States in 1884, worked with Edison and proposed wireless telegraphy before Marconi made it a reality. His patents made him rich and celebrated, but history has largely forgotten him, while elevating Thomas Edison and Guglielmo Marconi to the pantheon of great inventors. Tesla split with Edison because the American "wizard" insisted upon using direct current while Tesla wanted to explore the possibilities of alternating current. Tesla was correct, as Edison eventually realized. And while Marconi got the credit for discovering radio telegraphy in 1895, and successfully transmitted the first transatlantic signal in December 1901, Tesla had given a detailed lecture on the subject in St. Louis, Missouri, in 1893. Marconi always said that he knew nothing of Tesla's lecture, and it may be that it was one of those examples of concurrent discovery that regularly crop up in the history of science, an "idea whose time had come." The two men did sue each other several times over patents, but Tesla was not bitter about it. In *Tesla: Man Out of Time*, Margaret Cheney reported a conversation between Tesla and another of Edison's collaborators, H. Otis Pond, when Marconi's transatlantic signal was received. "Looks like Marconi got the jump on you," said Pond. "Marconi is a good fellow," Tesla replied. "Let him continue. His is using seven of my patents!"

Tesla's vision of what radio would do for the world was probably grander than Marconi's. He published an article in *Electrical World and Engineering* in 1904 in which he predicted that one day people would be able to carry portable receivers that "will record the world's news or such special messages as may be intended for it. Thus the entire earth will be converted into a huge brain, capable of response in every one of its parts." Not only was this prediction remarkable in terms of technological foresight, but it also prefigured by sixty years Marshall McLuhan's concept of a "global village" as set forth in *Understanding Media*. He could also have been speaking—even though he had no inkling of today's computer technology—of the world in the process of being created by the Internet and the World Wide Web.

1905 ▸ Women don't want to vote

Grover Cleveland

In 1905, former President Grover Cleveland made a pronouncement on the continuing agitation by the women's suffrage movement: "Sensible and responsible women do not want to vote. The relative positions to be assumed by man and woman in the working out of our civilization were assigned long ago by a higher intelligence than ours." The flagrant sexism of this statement infuriated many women even at the time, especially given Cleveland's personal history. During his first campaign for the presidency, in 1884, he had been accused of fathering a child out of wedlock. Unmarried, he admitted the fact. The public was thus given a choice between a man with "loose morals," and a Republican candidate, James G. Blaine, who had been charged with fraud in handling public money when he was a young politician. They chose the sexual offender, Cleveland. When he ran for reelection in 1888, he was beaten by Benjamin Harrison, but then unseated Harrison in 1892.

Cleveland's 1905 statement was actually just one more salvo in a war that had been going on for more than half a century. It had begun at the Seneca Falls Women's Rights Convention in 1848, even before the modern Republican party was born in the early 1850s. In 1878, California Senator Aaron A. Sargent introduced a Constitutional Amendment in Congress, stating: "The right of citizens of the United States to vote shall not be denied or abridged by the United States or by any states on account of sex." The same amendment, with the same language, was introduced in every new Congress for the following forty-two years. In the meantime, some modest success was achieved at the state level. Wyoming Territory gave women the vote in 1869, and continued to do so when it became a state in 1890. But the women of Wyoming still could not vote for president. Colorado followed suit in 1892. But it was not until 1917 that the first woman was elected to Congress, Jeanette Rankin of Montana. She immediately proved her mettle by being one of a handful of members of Congress to vote against the entry of the United States into World War I; a pacifist, she later was the only member of Congress to vote against entry into World War II following Pearl Harbor.

With the end of World War I, the time had finally arrived when women could no longer be denied the vote. On the 18th of August, 1920, the youngest member of the House of Representatives, twenty-four-year-old Harry Burn, cast the final vote for passage and cried out, "Hurrah! And vote for suffrage!" Famously, he voted yes because his mother told him to do so or else! President Wilson, who had long supported women's suffrage, declared the 19th Amendment ratified by proclamation on August 26. The right to vote did not change much for women in the short run, since the movement quickly fragmented, its moderate element led by the League of Women's Voters, and its more radical arm represented by the National Women's Party, headed by Alice Paul, which began lobbying for an Equal Rights Amendment that has failed to pass to this day. The first woman governor was Mrs. William B. Ross of Wyoming, elected to the post by the state legislature in 1925. It was not until 1974 that the nation had its first directly elected woman governor, Ella Grasso of Connecticut, with Geraldine A. Ferraro becoming the first woman to be nominated by a major party for Vice President in 1984.

1906 ▸ Cats know an earthquake is coming

Old wives' tale

At 5:13 A.M. on April 18, 1906, a massive earthquake hit San Francisco, California. The initial quake caused enormous damage, and the three days of fire that followed virtually destroyed the city. It was the most devastating earthquake in American history, leaving more than 200,000 people homeless. Numerous famous tales surrounded the awful event. Enrico Caruso had performed the previous evening, and barely escaped his collapsing hotel, vowing never again to set foot in the state of California. A young immigrant banker named Gianelli managed to get his small supply of gold out of the city to his farm in a vegetable wagon, and then set up business on the city's wharves, lending money to anyone with callused hands; out of that act of both generosity and good business sense he built a financial empire that would eventually become the Bank of America. In the aftermath new public health procedures were instituted to deal with an outbreak of bubonic plague, and new building methods and codes were developed to prevent future earthquakes from doing as much damage.

A small but curious side-story also developed. The press reported that many people claimed their cats had "gone crazy" shortly before the earthquake struck. Indeed, some people acquired cats as a kind of earthquake insurance. But scientists scoffed at the idea that cats would have any way of sensing that an earthquake was coming; "old wives' tales," they said. San Francisco suffered many lesser earthquakes over the ensuing decades, but then another big one struck before the second game of the 1989 World Series between the neighboring teams of the Oakland Athletics and the San Francisco Giants. Registering a 7.1 on the Richter scale, this one killed 60 people, destroyed highways, and riveted a nation tuning in for the game on television. And once again, in the aftermath, stories circulated about cats "going nuts" several minutes before anyone realized a major earthquake was about to take place. This time the scientists paid attention. People were awake instead of asleep, so there were more stories this time around about cats racing around rooms and shrieking hysterically. Moreover, the reports came not just from terrified "old wives," but from police officers, lab technicians, and others whose reports could not be so easily discounted. Seismologists decided that it was time to investigate the idea that cats might be able to sense the underground tremors before humans, or even machines, could. The results are not fully clear as yet. While cats do seem to be somewhat disturbed before mid-range earthquakes, it may be that it takes a major series of tremors to cause the severe reactions seen in 1989. If that is the case, when another big one strikes in California, scientists may know it is about to happen before their seismographs tell them it has started.

1908 ▶ An automobile for everybody

Henry Ford

Contrary to popular myth, Henry Ford didn't invent the automobile. There were "horseless buggies" in the 1880s, which were basically oversize tricycles with an engine attached. Nor did he invent the assembly line; that was done by his rival Ransom E. Olds. What Ford did do was to make full use of the idea of the assembly line to produce cars for average citizens. His earliest cars did not meet with much success, but with the N car of 1905 he began to hit his stride, and made a great leap forward in 1908 with the introduction of the Model T. In announcing this new vehicle, Ford said, "I am going to democratize the automobile, and when I'm through, everybody will be able to afford one, and about everybody will have one." This self-confident prediction was right on the mark.

The first model T sold for $850. There were a few cheaper cars on the market, from small companies, but most were several hundred dollars more. And the price of the Model T kept going down every year before reaching a low of $290 in 1923. Not only could most people afford them, but they became so popular that between 1908 and 1927 he sold 15.8 million of them. Ford stopped making the Model T in 1927 only because his competitors had forced his hand with cars that appealed more to the citizens of the Jazz Age. Ford had a stubborn streak, and he had refused to produce the Model T in anything but basic black, while his rivals introduced a wider range of colors. He also insisted on keeping the gas tank under the front seat, which meant that a cushion had to be moved to fill it up, an inconvenience other car makers got rid of by moving the tank to the rear.

Ford's son, Henry Ford II, inherited the old man's stubborn streak. Right after World War II, the younger Ford was offered the Volkswagen plant in Germany for free, if he would get it into production again. He refused, calling the Volkswagen beetle a "little shit box," and maintaining that it would never sell in America. The "Beetle" went on to become the only car to top the sales of the Model T, surpassing its total sales in 1972.

1910 Earth threatened by return of Halley's comet

Camille Flammarion

Edmund Halley not only made one of the most famous predictions in scientific history in connection with the comet that bears his name, but was also largely responsible for the fact that the name of Isaac Newton reverberates down the centuries as the discoverer of the laws of gravity. A mathematician and astronomer, Halley went to Newton in 1684 for help in working out the orbit of the great comet that had mesmerized scientists in 1682. From equations that Newton gave him, Halley recognized what Newton had accomplished in describing the effects of gravity on the orbits of the planets, and spent the next three years coaxing a manuscript on the subject out of the shy, retiring Newton. He edited the work and financed its publication in 1687, an act of friendship acknowledged by Newton in his preface. But Newton's orbital equations, and his identification of the elliptical nature of cometary paths, also gave Halley the tools he needed to calculate that the great comet of 1682 would return 76 years later, in 1759. The fame of each man was thus in large measure due to the other.

Halley's comet has indeed dutifully returned every 75 to 76 years, depending on how close it has passed Jupiter and Saturn, whose massive gravity impedes the comet's progress. But its appearance in 1910 brought forth another prediction, one that fortunately was not one for the ages. Astronomers had calculated that in 1910 the Earth would pass through the tail of Halley's comet for a six-hour period. Additional reports noted that the comet's tail contained, among many other components, cyanogen gas; this fact was reported on the front page of *The New York Times* on February 7, 1910, two months before the comet's appearance. As Richard Flaste, Holcomb Noble, Walter Sullivan, and John Nobel Wilford relate in their 1985 book, *The New York Times Guide to the Return of Halley's Comet*, the *Times* pointed out that cyanogen was a very deadly poison, going on to say, "The fact that cyanogen is present in the comet has been communicated to Camille Flammarion and many other astronomers, and is causing much discussion as to the probable effect on the Earth should it pass through the comet's tail. Prof. Flammarion is of the opinion that the cyanogen gas would impregnate the atmosphere and possibly snuff out all life on the planet."

Word of this threat spread rapidly. After all, if *The New York Times* said so. . . .

Camille Flammarion's prediction carried some genuine weight; he was in fact a distinguished astronomer at the Paris Observatory and had edited highly respected astronomical journals. His work on the influence of fluctuations in solar activity on plant and animal life on Earth was well known. But Flammarion was also given to doomsday scenarios. In 1893, for example, he had published a book called *La Fin du Monde* (*The End of the World*) suggesting that life on Earth would one day be wiped out by a collision with a comet. At the close of our own century, of course, such scenarios are again much in the news, due to strong evidence that the disappearance of the dinosaurs was due, at least in part, to the impact of an asteroid. But in 1910, no other scientists came forward to support Flammarion's prediction concerning the lethal effects of the cyanogen gas in the tail of Halley's comet. Several scientists, in fact, were quick to debunk the idea. *The Times*, having caused a good deal of anxiety with its front page story, published an editorial three days later giving the opinion of an American astronomer that the tails of comets were far too large and too tenuous to affect life on Earth even if they contained nothing but cyanogen gas.

But leashing in a scare story is much harder than letting it out of the kennel to begin with, and the rumor that Halley's comet was going to destroy life on Earth was already beyond control. There was considerable panic in a number of cities around the world; Chicago became the hot spot in the United States. There the newspapers carried reports of people stuffing towels into the cracks under doors, and of physicians treating numerous cases of hysteria as the comet made its closest approach to Earth on May 18.

Professor Flammarion was, of course, completely wrong. There was, however, one significant death connected with the 1910 passage of Halley's comet across the heavens, that of Mark Twain. The most famous American writer of his time had had several heart attacks in 1901, and had written, "I came in with Halley's comet in 1835. It is coming again next year, and I expect to go out with it. It will be the greatest disappointment of my life if I don't. The almighty has said, no doubt: 'Now here are these two unaccountable freaks; they came in together, they must go out together.' Oh, I am looking forward to that."

Halley's comet had its brightest moment as it wheeled around the sun on April 20, 1910. Mark Twain died the following day.

1910 No transatlantic airplane passenger service

William H. Pickering

In 1910, the eminent American astronomer William H. Pickering wrote, "The popular mind often pictures gigantic flying machines speeding across the Atlantic and carrying innumerable passengers in a way analogous to our modern steamships. . . . It seems safe to say that such ideas must be wholly visionary, and even if a machine could get across with one or two passengers the expense would be prohibitive to any but the capitalist who could own his own yacht." This statement is so short-sighted as to appear reactionary. After all, the Wright brothers had first flown seven years earlier, and had begun building planes for the U.S. Army in 1907. They, and other aviation pioneers, particularly in Europe, were improving the range and stability of planes year by year. True, they were still small one-or two-seaters, but given the fact that right up to the moment that the Wrights had their first success at Kitty Hawk self-appointed "experts" were saying flight was impossible, one would think Pickering might have thought it better to keep his opinion to himself.

Arthur C. Clarke has said that people who scoff at future possibilities in fields other than their own are always wrong. But it is also true that people who *do* entertain fantastic developments in fields other than their can be correct. One of the first to make the comparison between sea-vessels and air-vessels, which Pickering ascribed to "the popular mind," was none other than the great English poet, Lord Byron. And he did it eighty-eight years earlier, in 1822. "I suppose," he wrote, "we shall soon travel by air-vessels; make air instead of sea-voyages; and at length find out way to the moon, in spite of the want of atmosphere." Of course, Lord Byron was not just a great poet, but also a great adventurer. Perhaps most important, he had an epic imagination, which is often far more important in grasping the possibilities of the future than the scientific knowledge of conservative thinkers like Pickering.

It did, however, take some time for transatlantic passenger service to be established. It was inaugurated in June 1939, with a flight from New York to England. In *The 20th Century*, David Wallechinsky writes, "The fare one way was $375, round trip $675—no more than a first-class fare on an ocean liner at the time." Pickering had been wrong on that point also.

1912 ▸ The *Titanic* unsinkable

Word of mouth

Michael Davie, author of *Titanic: The Death and Life of a Legend*, made a particular effort to track down how the great ocean liner acquired its reputation as being unsinkable before its tragic maiden voyage. "I found it hard to believe that anyone, even at the height of

Edwardian self-confidence, could have believed in the possibility of an 'unsinkable' ship, least of all the hard and experienced shipbuilders and shipowners of Belfast and Liverpool." He found a reference to the ship as being "practically unsinkable" in a shipping journal, and a pamphlet published after the sinking that claimed the owners had used the same words in describing the watertight doors to him. But the general public did not read shipping journals, and the pamphlet was published after the fact. Even so, "Time and again at the official inquiries passengers and crew testified that they had reacted slowly to the collision because they thought the *Titanic* unsinkable."

We are obviously dealing here with one of those situations in which the public makes an assumption and repeats it so often in conversation that it becomes an accepted fact. This is the word-of-mouth realm of rumor and gossip in which people come to believe things—sometimes quite outlandish things—regardless of the truth. But to have believed the *Titanic* unsinkable was not at all strange. Its double bottom and watertight doors were much touted, and in an age of grandeur, its sheer size (although the *Queen Elizabeth II* would eventually be even bigger) and opulence suggested a ship that even nature at her angriest could not intimidate.

White Star Line's *Titanic* would of course go down all too easily, in less than two hours after it struck an iceberg off Newfoundland on April 14–15, 1912 with a loss of 1,522 lives. But as reported in April 1997 by *The New York Times* and on a Discovery Channel two-hour special, undersea tests of the ship's wreckage with sonar equipment in the summer of 1996 revealed that its sinking was due to greater bad luck than had ever been realized before. It had long been believed by most experts that the bow had suffered a 300-foot gash covering six of the ship's supposedly watertight compartments. But the sound wave tests in 1996 found only six small openings, totaling a mere 12 to 13 square feet, in the hull. It was not the size of these openings but their placement that spelled doom for the great liner. It is still agreed that the ship was going too fast at an estimated 22 knots for the icy waters it was traversing, but if the small holes that were slashed in the hull had been concentrated on a smaller area, the ship might have survived. As it was, the public belief that the *Titanic* was unsinkable made the tragedy even greater because passengers and crew were so slow to react.

1912 The discovery of the previous existence of a single supercontinent

Alfred Wegener

In 1912, the geologist Alfred Wegener claimed that the existing continents had once comprised a single, enormous land mass that he called Pangea, a word derived from the Greek and meaning "all earth." This claim represents a special category of prediction, in which a previously unconsidered past condition or event is set forth as a truth yet to be proved. Another example would be the theory that the dinosaurs were wiped out by the catastrophic consequences of a huge asteroid hitting the Earth (see 1980). Wegener's claim was based on the revolutionary concept of continental drift, which held that the Earth's land masses were in constant, if almost imperceptible, motion, carried on thin plates on the surface of the earth.

People were still getting used to the concept of plate tectonics, and many dismissed Wegener's idea as fanciful nonsense on a par with the existence of the lost continent of Atlantis, originally presented as "hearsay" by Plato. Nevertheless, there were enough geologists who took Wegener seriously, and evidence to support his theory was noted when it cropped up. It took almost seventy years to amass sufficient data, but by the 1980s, rock formations around the world had yielded up truly hard evidence that Wegener had been right. From the start, it had been clear, simply by looking at a flat map of the earth's surface, that the present continents did in many places look like scattered pieces of a jigsaw puzzle, with South America in particular fitting neatly into the west coast of Africa. But it was only when the rocks found on separate continents could be shown to have once been of a single geological nature that the theory was proven conclusively.

By the 1980s, it was in fact possible to make a coherent map of Pangea as it existed 200 million years ago. That success led to ideas that an even earlier supercontinent, named Rodinia after the Russian word for "motherland," had come apart some 500 million years ago and then reformed to make up Pangea itself. Further investigation and research has provided evidence to support the reality of Rodinia. Some geologists, particularly John Rogers of the University of North Carolina, are now speculating on the existence of separate continents that even preceded Rodinia. But it was Alfred Wegener who made the initial daring intellectual leap that has so drastically altered our understanding of the globe we live on.

1912 ▶ The "missing link" found

Charles Dawson

One of the many legacies of Charles Darwin and his theory of evolution was to inspire thousands of amateur geologists to hunt for fossilized bones that would provide further proof of his ideas. Of particular interest was the matter of the "missing link," bones that would pinpoint the existence of a creature halfway between the surviving apes and the remains of such early men as the Neanderthals. We know now that the apes are our cousins rather than our direct predecessors, but in the year 1912 the hunt was on for bones that could be identified as a clear half man–half ape intermediary. Charles Dawson, a lawyer with a great interest in geology, thought that he found exactly that when he unearthed a skull in a gravel bed near Lewes, England. The skull was unlike anything seen before, combining a clearly human cranium with an apelike jaw. Because it had been found on Piltdown Common, this supposed representative of the missing link was dubbed Piltdown Man.

Tests by the world's foremost experts attested to the authenticity of the skull. Scientists were dismayed that thorough searches of the area around Lewes were unable to turn up any other such skulls, but a wide variety of excuses were devised to account for the singular survival to modern times of Dawson's find. Piltdown Man went into the biology textbooks, and was a widely cited riposte to creationist claims that man, in the form of Adam, had been created by God only a few thousand years earlier. It was not until forty years later that new methods of chemical analysis were used on the Piltdown skull. To the horror of scientists, it was found that their missing link consisted of a human cranium attached to an orangutan's jaw. The job had been done with great skill, but the headlines now screamed PILTDOWN HOAX! Some scientists had suspected as much for some time, which was why the skull had been subjected to new tests, but the entire affair was a great embarrassment to science.

The hoax was revealed in 1953, 41 years after the discovery of the skull; it would take another 43 to discover who had perpetrated it. In the intervening years, attempting to unmask the hoaxer became a cottage industry, like uncovering the identity of Jack the Ripper or the "real" Shakespeare. Dozens of suspects were put forward by enterprising researchers. Because he had found the skull, Charles Dawson was a primary suspect, but no one could demonstrate that he had the skills to put together such a convincing forgery. Finally, after a decade of amassing evidence, two British paleontologists, Brian Gardiner and Andrew Currant, announced in 1996 that they had nailed the culprit. An old trunk found at the British Museum had provided the first crucial evidence; it contained bones that had, like the Piltdown skull, been dipped in acid and treated with manganese and iron oxides. As reported in *Discover* magazine, the trunk was inscribed with the initials M.A.C.H., those of the keeper of zoology at the British Museum from the mid-1930s to the mid-1940s, whose last name was Hinton. Gardiner and Currant were able to come up with other evidence that supplied a motive. As a young man working as a volunteer at the museum, Hinton had been contemptuously refused a salary by the then keeper of paleontology, Arthur Smith Woodward. The construction of Piltdown Man was an all too successful attempt to embarrass Woodward. And since Hinton went on to become a respected scientist himself, it became impossible to admit to the hoax. Whether Hinton deliberately left the trunk as evidence of his "crime" is impossible to know. But even in his lifetime, he had planted a clue in his entry for the British *Who's Who*. Among his interests, he included "hoaxes."

1913 ► An airplane in every garage

Waldemar Kaempfert

The airplane had been around for a decade in 1913, and continuing improvements suggested that it was here to stay. Many people who should have known better still couldn't grasp its real potential, however, doubting that it would have much military use or that it could ever supplant trains and ocean liners as a form of transportation. There were those who went too far in the other direction, though. One such futurist was the managing editor of *Scientific American*, Waldemar Kaempfert. He wrote, "Over cities . . . the aerial sentry or policeman will be found. A thousand aeroplanes flying to the opera must be kept in line and each allowed to alight upon the roof of the auditorium in its proper turn."

Kaempfert must be given credit for being one of the first to foresee the need for air-traffic controllers, but beyond that he was a trifle overexcited. All of New York City's Lincoln Center for the Performing Arts wouldn't provide nearly enough space to park a thousand airplanes, let alone land them, not even the small one- and two-seaters of those days. And while Henry Ford's Model T automobile was falling in price every year and thus becoming the property of Everyman, it was a major leap to imagine a plane in every garage, or at least the garages of everyone who could afford to go the opera. Today there are enough private planes to give air-controllers the willies, and helicopters do wondrously land on the roofs of buildings, but the vision of a thousand planes flying in to make an 8:00 o'clock curtain remains in the realm of the most boyish kind of science fiction. Still, it's an endearing idea, right up there with Han Solo having his own beat-up spaceship in *Star Wars*.

1913 ▶ Atomic bombs

H. G. Wells

The phrase "atomic bombs" was coined by H. G. Wells in his 1913 novel, *The World Set Free*, set in the far-off 1950s. The bombs themselves were like large grenades, with a fuse that aviators bit off before dropping them out of the cockpits of their planes. Wells's lack of imagination in terms of the development of aircraft is surprising, but not only was he the first one to refer to atomic bombs, he also was correct in surmising that a single such device could destroy an entire city.

Wells's ideas on atomic bombs were derived directly from the work of Ernest Rutherford and Frederick Soddy, who discovered at the end of 1901 that radioactivity was a sign of fundamental change—the atoms of one element, radioactive thorium, changing into radium atoms. Frederick Soddy had a more utopian outlook than Rutherford, writing in his 1908 book, *The Interpretation of Radium*, that the "transmutation" of the energy within atoms "could transform a desert continent, thaw the frozen poles, and make the whole world one smiling Garden of Eden." But he had also written in 1903 that his and Rutherford's discoveries had revealed that the planet was "a storehouse stuffed with explosives, inconceivably more powerful than any we know of, and possibly only awaiting a suitable detonator to cause the earth to revert to chaos."

Wells, who was both a social critic and a utopian dreamer, drew on both these strands in *The World Set Free*, which was dedicated to Frederick Soddy. The use of atomic bombs in the novel, based on the explosive potential of transmuting the atom, nearly destroys civilization but thus brings the human race to its senses, so that it creates a new world government that uses atomic power to transform both deserts and polar regions into the kinds of edens Soddy had suggested. Unfortunately, the coinage of the term *atomic bombs* has proved the realistic prophecy.

1914 ▸ Planes will prevent war

Claude Graham-White and Harry Harper

On the eve of the First World War, the British aviators Claude Graham-White and Harry Harper held out the hope that airplanes, even if they could not prevent imminent hostilities, would eventually serve to bring about a lasting peace between nations. "First Europe," they wrote, "and then the globe, will be linked by flight, and nations so knit together that they will grow to be next-door neighbors." Planes were not, in fact, a major combat weapon during World War I, but the first dogfights between planes with crudely mounted machine guns did take place, as did the first bombing attempts. By 1917, Orville Wright would set down the following rueful words: "When my brother and I built and flew the first man-carrying machine, we thought that we were introducing into the world an invention that would make further wars impossible."

The idea that closer connections and better knowledge of other people will pave the way to peace has been treasured by idealists since the beginning of recorded history, of course, but the naiveté of the Wright brothers and of Graham-White and Harper remains surprising. After all, even hot air balloons had long since been put into action in military conflicts. The first air raid in world history had taken place in 1849, when the Austrians used pilotless balloons to bomb Venice. Gas balloons were used during the Civil War by the Union army as reconnaissance vehicles to keep track of Confederate troop movements. In fact, President Lincoln himself had approved funds for balloon construction after attending a demonstration by the inventor and aerialist Thaddeus C. Lowe of Connecticut. The Confederates, in an attempt to match this new technology, had constructed and launched a balloon made from silk ball gowns donated by wealthy women from all over the South. This resplendent creation was, of course, visible for miles, and was brought down by the Union forces within an hour. One Confederate general was so incensed by this insult to Southern womanhood that he was still complaining about it twenty years later.

With these, and many other, examples of the potential wartime use of vehicles that could be sent aloft, it is astonishing that the military possibilities of airplanes were not very much in the minds of the Wrights and other pioneers of motorized flight. In fact, Orville Wright may have been protesting too much in 1917. The Wrights had begun building experimental planes for the U.S. Army as early as 1908, although it is true that the army represented the only possible commercial contract they could get at the time.

1915 The existence of a ninth planet

Percival Lowell

The astronomer Percival Lowell, who had been so wrong about the Martian canals he had claimed to see in 1894, was right about many other things. Most famously, he predicted the existence of the ninth planet, which we call Pluto. Perturbations in the orbits of Neptune and Uranus led him to the conclusion that their orbits must be affected by the gravitational pull of an as yet undiscovered body at the outer edges of the solar system. Lowell dubbed this body Planet X, and published his final calculations on where it might be found in 1915, the year before his death. Another Bostonian, William Pickering, had been working on the same problem independently. When he updated his own calculations concerning the location of what he called Planet O, in 1919, he also suggested that there might be still another body, which he labeled Planet S, orbiting the sun.

Lowell had called for the construction of a special wide-field camera to aid in the search for his Planet X. It was finally put into operation at the Lowell Observatory, at Flagstaff, Arizona, in 1929. Percival Lowell had helped to fund the construction of the observatory with his own fortune, and was in charge of it during his lifetime. The techniques for using the new wide-field camera were developed by Clyde W. Tombaugh, who finally identified Lowell's predicted planet on February 18, 1930. The planet was named Pluto, which not only maintained the use of names from Roman mythology, but also memorialized Percival Lowell in its first two letters.

Lowell had been wrong about what he thought he had actually seen with his own eyes, the canals of Mars, but right about what he couldn't see, the ninth planet. But is it, in fact, a planet? Questions about that have since been raised. Not only is it very small, it has since been discovered that it does not have sufficient mass to affect the orbits of Neptune and Uranus. Some astronomers believe it may actually be a one-time moon of Neptune, whose orbit Pluto crosses inside during its 240-year period of rotation around the sun. On the other hand, it was discovered in 1978 that Pluto has a satellite of its own, which was called Charon, after the boatman who in Greek mythology ferries the dead across to the god Pluto's underworld realm. Could both Pluto and Charon be former moons of Neptune?

There have also been speculations that William Pickering was right, and that still another planet, as yet undiscovered, orbits the sun still farther out, or perhaps on a trajectory that keeps it permanently hidden from us on the other side of the sun. At any rate, a gravitational mystery remains, one that cannot be clarified, as were perturbations in the orbit of Mercury, by Einstein's theory of relativity. Something else has to be out there. Nevertheless, Pluto did exist where Lowell said it would, and that in itself stands as a major triumph in the history of astronomical predictions.

1916 ▶ The sun not at the center of the galaxy

Harlow Shapley

In the early years of this century, the Harvard College Observatory Office in Cambridge, Massachusetts, employed a number of women to sort, categorize, and label the thousands of plates taken at the Harvard College Observatory in Peru. These women were known by the nickname "the computers." Astronomy was then an all-male preserve, but the exacting, tedious work these women did was essential to the theoretical work done by the astronomers themselves. Among these remarkable women, the standout was Henrietta Swan Leavitt. In 1912, in the course of categorizing plates taken of the Magellanic Clouds, Leavitt realized that the differences in what were called Cepheid stars were accounted for by their size, or magnitude, rather than distance alone. Some were brighter because they were closer to the Earth, while others were brighter because they were so large. This discovery led to the basis for measuring the distance of stars from our own solar system.

Leavitt's discovery led to many breakthroughs in astronomy, but none was more important than that made by Harlow Shapley. With this new tool of measurement at hand, Shapley made a study of the globular clusters in the Milky Way Galaxy (which at the time was believed to be the only galaxy), using the 60-inch reflecting telescope at Mt. Wilson in Pasadena, California. From these studies he made what Timothy Ferris describes in his book *Coming of Age in the Milky Way* as a "superbly daring intuitive leap." Almost all astronomers believed that our sun was near or at the center of the galaxy, but Shapley saw that this was wrong, and that we were in fact located on the outskirts of the galaxy. (Freud, at about the same time, was noting that all great breakthroughs in human knowledge served to knock humankind off the self-important pedestal on which it liked to believe it was standing.) Shapley estimated that our solar system lay about 50,000 light years from the center. This distance was later corrected to 30,000 light years; Shapley had made a mistake because he had overestimated the size of the Milky Way on the assumption that it was the sole galaxy.

But the very idea that we were located on the outskirts of the Milky Way was revolutionary. It was fiercely resisted by some astronomers, but was the impetus needed to lead others in new directions. Edwin Hubble, for whom the space telescope is named, was the first astronomer to make it clear, in a paper delivered in Washington, D.C., on New Year's Day of 1925, that there were multitudes of galaxies or "island universes." Shapley himself built on that idea with his further studies of the Magellanic Clouds, finding that other galaxies tended to occur in clusters, which he called metagalaxies. Shapley was director of the Harvard College Observatory from 1920 to 1952, and continued to do important work into his eighties. By relocating the sun, he opened the way to the vast reaches of space and time that we have since come to recognize.

1916 ◢ Matter warps space

Albert Einstein

Does the earth have an outer edge? People believed that it did for centuries; if you went beyond it, you'd fall off. Does the universe have an outer edge? That question, too, goes back to the ancient Greeks, particularly Plato's colleague, Archytas the Pythagorean. Albert Einstein's General Theory of Relativity finally gave a solution to this problem when it was published in the spring of 1916. The theory showed how the universe could contain a finite number of stars in a finite amount of space, but still not be "closed" or have an edge one could fall off, as it were. Einstein demonstrated mathematically that matter warps space. In the process, the galaxies would be wrapped around one another to form a sphere, so that if one could travel far enough fast enough one would eventually return to one's starting point, just as on the Earth itself. If that was too simple, the universe could also have a hyperbolic form, but that, too, could be traversed in a way that returned one to the starting point.

Einstein's mathematics were of an awesome beauty. Physicists wanted to believe them. But would they hold up if they were tested against some observable event? The chance to make such a proof came three years later, when a solar eclipse would occur on May 29, 1919, observable only from the southern hemisphere. The British astronomer, Arthur Stanley Eddington, organized an expedition to Principe Island, which lies off the west coast of equatorial Africa. If Einstein was right, the briefly darkened sky ought to reveal a distortion in the apparent position of the stars. And, indeed, Eddington's experiment, as well as another conducted simultaneously in Brazil, found that the distortion not only existed but conformed almost exactly to the degree predicted by the theory.

The confirmation of his theory almost immediately made Einstein the most famous scientist on earth, and he went on to become a beloved public figure. But Einstein was not quite as cuddly as the public liked to believe, and was certainly not given to false modesty. When asked what he would have done if Eddington's expedition had failed to prove the theory of relativity correct, Einstein replied, "I would have had to pity our dear Lord. The theory is correct."

1917 The shortening of the Mississippi River

Mark Twain

In the posthumously published *Life on the Mississippi*, Mark Twain wrote, "In the space of one hundred and seventy-six years the Lower Mississippi has shortened itself two hundred and forty-two miles. That is an average of a trifle over one mile and a third a year. Therefore, any calm person, who is not blind or idiotic, can see that in the Old Oolitic Silurian Period, just a million years ago next November, the Lower Mississippi River was upward of one million three hundred miles long, and stuck out over the Gulf of Mexico like a fishing-rod. And by the same token any person can see that seven hundred and forty-two years from now the Lower Mississippi will be only a mile and three-quarters long, and Cairo (Illinois) and New Orleans will have joined their streets together, and be plodding comfortably along under a single mayor and a mutual board of aldermen. There is something fascinating about science. One gets such wholesale returns of conjecture out of such a trifling investment of fact."

Mark Twain specialized in this kind of joke, sending up the human tendency to draw sweeping conclusions from circumscribed data. He would have gotten a great kick out of the bizarre implications of today's quantum physics. For example, a major science story in *The New York Times* in February 1997 focused on new findings about the supposed vacuum of space. It turns out that it is not really a vacuum after all. Instead it is full of subatomic particles that pop in and out of reality, apparently at whim; for a microsecond they are there, and then they disappear again. For infinitesimal amounts of time, they inhabit our "reality" and then zip off to some other plane of time and space. This in itself sounds ridiculous, but the strange behavior of subatomic particles has been empirically established beyond question. Some scientists, however, take things several steps further. Since the vacuum of space isn't one, and since there are particles that pop in and out of existence on an intermittent basis, the suggestion has been made that the vacuum we know could collapse into a "purer" one. If so, all present matter in the universe, including our Milky Way Galaxy, our solar system, and, of course, ourselves, would wink out of existence so quickly that we wouldn't even know it had happened.

This possibility was first put forward in 1982, in an article in *Nature* by the physicists Michael S. Turner and Frank Wilczek. It has been contested by some other physicists, but is certainly considered a possibility. And while Mark Twain might well consider this an example of getting "such wholesale returns of conjecture out of such a trifling investment of fact," it is also likely that he would have been fascinated by the idea. Twain had a very dark and sinister side to his imagination, chiefly expressed in lesser known works like *The Mysterious Stranger*, and might not have been all that averse to considering the collapse of the universe, however put out he was about the dwindling of his beloved Mississippi.

1920 ▸ Rockets won't work in space

The New York Times

Robert H. Goddard, for whom the Goddard Space Center was later named, was born in 1882. He was one of the great pioneers in the field of rocketry, but for much of his life he was derided for his work. As William B. Breuer puts it in *Race to the Moon*, "In 1919, he wrote a document called *A Method of Reaching Extreme Altitudes*, which presented formulas for computing the power necessary to put a rocket on the moon. America yawned and branded Goddard as a hare-brained crackpot." One of the name-callers, the *New York Times*, published an editorial lambasting Goddard himself, Clark University in Massachusetts, where he was a professor, and the Smithsonian Institution, which had expressed interest in his work. The editorial said his ideas were absurd since the vacuum of space would provide nothing against which a rocket could react to provide thrust. The *Times* concluded, "Of course he only seems to lack the knowledge ladled out daily in high schools."

But Goddard kept experimenting, and if he was regarded as a crackpot in his own country, others began to recognize the importance of his work. In 1936, a German spy named Gustave Guellich, who worked in the laboratories of a U.S. Steel subsidiary in New Jersey as a metallurgist, was dispatched by the Nazis to New Mexico to clandestinely watch the launching of one of Goddard's experimental rockets. The rocket, Breuer writes, "was controlled by a gyroscope and by vanes in the exhaust system. It rose to an altitude of 4,800 feet, swung to horizontal flight in response to its steering mechanism, reached a speed of 550 miles per hour, and continued for nearly three miles before plunging to earth." Guellich reported to Berlin that Goddard had made "a substantial breakthrough in the development of rocket-propelled missiles."

Goddard's ideas were used in the development of Germany's V-2 rockets, and after World War II, German rocket scientists, including Wernher von Braun were brought to the United States to work in the American rocket program. As for the *New York Times*, it eventually did the right thing. A month before Apollo 11 landed on the moon, the *Times* published a formal retraction of its 1920 editorial attacking Robert H. Goddard.

1921 ⯈ Ships can't be bombed from the air

Newton D. Baker

Newton D. Baker was President Warren Harding's secretary of war, a fairly distinguished member of a notoriously second-rate cabinet. But he was hardly alone in his resistance to the idea that air power was the wave of the future. The great American champion of air power in the aftermath of the First World War was an American army general, born William Mitchell but always called Billy Mitchell. His army career had begun as a private in the infantry during the Spanish American War of 1898. He subsequently served in several foreign locales, and graduated from the Army Staff College in 1909. An early enthusiast of airplanes, he became an extremely successful air commander during World War I, rising to head a French-American force of nearly 1,500 planes.

Following the war, he was appointed second-in-command of the air services branch of the U.S. Army. It was in this position that he had the idea of demonstrating the importance of air power by bombing a captured or retired battleship. War Secretary Baker thought this was ridiculous. "That idea is so damned nonsensical and impossible," he told the press, "that I'm willing to stand on the bridge of a battleship while some nitwit tries to hit it from the air." The nitwit he was referring to, Billy Mitchell, persevered, and made so much noise that the demonstration was finally allowed in order to shut him and the press up. Held in July 1921, it was a complete success, sinking a captured German battleship. Secretary of War Baker was not, however, present on the bridge.

Billy Mitchell was one of the first and most outspoken advocates of a separate U.S. Air Force, an idea that both the army and the navy fought to the bitter end. In 1925 he was reassigned to an almost invisible post in San Antonio, Texas. Later that year, when a navy dirigible, the *Shenandoah*, was lost in a storm, Mitchell, who felt it should not have been aloft in such weather, accused the war and navy departments of "criminal negligence." He was court-martialed and convicted, and he resigned from the army. He remained a great hero to those who backed air power, however. He died in 1936, before World War II completely vindicated his views on the importance of aerial bombing, but he had become such a popular hero that

Hollywood produced a movie starring Gary Cooper called *The Court Martial of Billy Mitchell*. In 1946, Congress voted to issue a special medal in his honor, and the separate air force he had called for came into being in 1948.

1921 ▶ Robots

Karel Capek

In 1921 a play called *R.U.R.* was first performed in Prague, capital of the newly created country of Czechoslovakia. An instant success, it was translated into numerous languages and performed across Europe, in England, and in the United States.

Its author, Karel Capek, was the art director of the National Theater of Prague, but beyond that he was a man with an astonishing range of interests and talents who wrote not only plays and novels but also widely read travel and gardening books. Although his novel *The War with the Newts* is still in print around the world, he is most famous for *R.U.R.*, in which he invented the word *robot*, based on a Slavic root for "work." R.U.R. stood for "Rossum's Universal Robots," soulless artificial beings with a blank humanoid appearance. Although manufactured, Kopek's robots were biological creations akin to those in the 1982 cult movie *Blade Runner*, which was developed from Philip K. Dick's 1968 novel *Do Androids Dream of Electric Sleep?* The word *robot* had become reserved for machines (or creatures, in fiction) made of metal by the mid-1930s. Capek's robots would be called androids or even clones today, but the idea of man-made creatures designed to carry out menial, repetitive, or dangerous tasks under the control of humans was entirely his. In the 1940s, Isaac Asimov codified the robotic tribe with the "Three Laws of Robotics" he developed with input from John W. Campbell, editor of *Astounding Science Fiction*.

Humanoid robots, whether of metal or flesh, have not yet, of course, become a reality. Computerized metal robots are widely used in industry and scientific research, but they remain highly specialized machines, often consisting primarily of arms. Many experimental robots capable of moving around on their own have been built, but they remain far from humanoid in appearance.

By mid-century Capek's biological robots seemed far more fanciful than metal varieties. But many scientists now believe that the fastest developing field over the next several decades will be that of genetic engineering. If that proves true, then some combination of biological material, plastics, and metal may yet be created in humanoid form in the next century—which would be right in line with the fictional androids of numerous writers who have drawn on both Capek's and Asimov's ideas.

It should be remembered, however, that Capek's original robots wiped out humanity. Capek's play was both a satire on capitalism run amok and a warning about how automation could bring about our own dehumanization. In the 1990s, these themes have every bit as much resonance as his invention of the word *robot*.

1922 Motion pictures will replace books as school texts

Thomas Edison

In 1922, Thomas Edison said, "I believe that the motion picture is destined to revolutionize our educational system and that in a few years it will supplant largely, if not entirely, the use of textbooks." As one of the major patent holders on motion-picture technology, Edison, of course, had a vested interest in just such a development. Even so, on the surface this seems like a perfectly sensible prediction. The reasons why it didn't come true provide an object lesson in the realities that can undermine the potentials for any new technology.

It should be noted at the outset that Edison didn't even finish high school, and had little appreciation of the formal educational process. He was a genius, one of the great self-starters of all time, and really had no need for formal education. But very few schoolchildren are geniuses or self-starters—they need constant supervision in order to learn. It is a truism of education, shown in thousands of studies, that children and teenagers require a considerable degree of individual attention. The more students in a class, the less they learn. There are debates about the ideal teacher-student ratio, but it is abundantly clear that when a single teacher has more than thirty students, the educational process begins to fall apart; the teacher becomes a babysitter or room monitor instead of an instructor. Yet the economics of using film or video to teach demand that there be fewer teachers in order to afford the hardware for showing the films and renting or buying the instruction materials.

The supposed solution was to have the teacher on the film, but that made it impossible to answer questions, reiterate facts that hadn't been grasped, or simply to keep order.

Until the VCR came along, the only way to use film was to show it to large groups. This sometimes meant a field trip to a theater to see, say, a Shakespeare film, but that involved the expense of buses for transportation and paying the theater owner, even at a reduced rate. School time was also lost in effecting such a mass migration. Thus it was far more common to show films at assemblies in the auditorium on the school property. But that brought its own problems. This writer attended Phillips Academy in Andover, Massachusetts, where there was a school assembly every Wednesday morning, at which films were often shown. One memorable Wednesday, one of the films Leonard Bernstein had made for television to explain music for young people was shown. Early in the film, he demonstrated conducting technique, starting with the downbeat and the upbeat of the baton. Laughter began almost at once, and then those who were laughing whispered to their neighbors that the whole thing sounded like a lesson in how to masturbate. Within a minute, there were 900 teenage boys laughing hysterically. The film had to be shut off, and the school dean read us the riot act, although most of the faculty members present couldn't immediately figure out what the ruckus was about. This may be a somewhat extreme example, but it does indicate the problem involved in showing large numbers of teenagers an "instructive" film.

As television made its way into almost every American home, teachers sometimes tried to assign a particularly instructive television program as homework. But there were other people at home who might not want to watch that program, and the student might also want to watch something more popular that was on at the same time. The VCR made it possible to view a tape at any hour, and the rewind button could be used by the dedicated student to go back over something he or she didn't fully understand. But that's the dedicated student; more were likely to use the fast forward button and others wouldn't watch at all. Never mind the expense of providing everyone with videotapes.

And so Edison was wrong. Film did not even begin to replace textbooks. There are now those who see the Internet as replacing textbooks, but maybe they should think again.

1924 ▶ No talking in movies

D. W. Griffith

In 1924, the *Saturday Evening Post* rounded up important figures in many fields and asked them to predict what the world would be like 100 years in the future. Since the magazine was a resolutely status-quo publication, the editors chose rather conservative people to do the predicting, and nothing too outlandish was suggested. To comment on the future of movies, the great director D. W. Griffith was chosen. Although he had played a major role in elevating the silent film into an art form, with such famous features as *Birth of a Nation* (1915) and *Intolerance* (1916), Griffith was a social conservative—his positive treatment of the Ku Klux Klan in *Birth of a Nation* was controversial from the start. In his contribution to the *Post*, he wrote, "We do not want now and we shall never want the human voice with our films." That "we" meant everyone, of course—Griffith was never known for his modesty.

Since Griffith was a master of the silent form, understanding how to elicit powerful audience reactions without resorting to spoken dialogue, his failure to see that the public would be thrilled by the advent of sound was hardly surprising. But three years later his view was echoed by the president of Warner Brothers Pictures, Harry M. Warner, who exclaimed, "Who the hell wants to hear actors talk?" It's remarkable that such resistance came from Harry Warner, since it had been his own studio that had introduced the sound-on-disc Vitaphone process to movies the previous year in *Don Juan*. But this process was seen as saving money; the disc could be played in theaters instead of hiring a pianist in smaller theaters, or a full orchestra in big-city movie palaces. In fact, Warner's statement was in reaction to pressure from Al Jolson to have spoken dialogue in *The Jazz Singer*, in which there was to be a Vitaphone soundtrack for several Jolson songs. But in a recording session, Jolson snuck in the words "Wait a minute. Wait a minute. You ain't heard nothing yet," and the sound era was born. Audiences went wild, and the other major studios immediately jumped on the bandwagon.

The introduction of sound did bring a lot of problems, however. Some were technical. Directors had to figure out how to keep actors near the primitive microphones without bringing movement to a total halt. The sound itself was initially scratchy and patchy, even after the technology was developed to put the sound track directly on the film. Most dismaying, it was quickly apparent that many major stars would be lost to the new medium. Heavy accents, whether from Europe or Brooklyn, were one problem, and high-pitched male voices or flat female ones were often at odds with a star's visual image. A few stars, most notably Garbo, whose low-pitched voice and seductive accent perfectly matched her screen persona, triumphed in sound pictures. But a whole new group of stars, from Bette Davis and Henry Fonda to Irene Dunne and Fredric March, had to be brought in from Broadway and molded into movie icons.

There were those who resisted sound no matter what audiences seemed to want. The one who managed to get away with it longest was Charlie Chaplin, who said in 1928, "Moving pictures need sound as much as Beethoven symphonies need lyrics." He stuck to his guns with *City Lights* (1931) and *Modern Times* (1936), using music and sound effects but almost no dialogue. There were also those among the critics who thought something was lost with the transition to sound. To this day, some will say that no sound picture ever equaled the pictorial montage achieved in the last of the great silents, King Vidor's *The Crowd*, which was released in 1928. Vidor went on to make many important sound pictures, but *The Crowd* remained his masterpiece. D. W. Griffith was completely wrong in saying that *we* didn't want talkies, but there were good reasons why he—and Chaplin and Vidor and others— didn't want them. Those directors knew how to make masterpieces without sound.

1927 ► Radiology shops in every neighborhood

J. B. S. Haldane

J. B. S. Haldane was a biologist—and a fervent Marxist—who wrote many best-selling books popularizing science and linking new discoveries to a vastly improved world for the masses. He was particularly enthusiastic about the medical use of radiation, and in a 1927 book called *Possible Worlds and Other Essays*, predicted that radiology shops would eventually become as common as local pharmacies, with technicians using various combinations of rays to treat numerous physical ailments.

At the time Haldane's prediction was really just an extrapolation of medical procedures that already existed. The use of radioactivity in place of surgery to destroy some kinds of tumors had already been pioneered, and the use of X rays as a diagnostic tool was becoming commonplace. By the mid-1930s, more than 25 million patients were being X-rayed around the world every year. At the same time, however, it was already known when Haldane made his prophecy that radiation could be dangerous in excessive amounts. Incidents involving the deaths of scientists and technicians from radiation poisoning or cancers induced by long-term exposure had been well-publicized in the press. But the very fact that these were people who worked with radiation on a daily basis quelled the fears of ordinary citizens, and the clear medical usefulness of X rays as well as the cures effected by radiation treatment more than counterbalanced any horror stories. It was not until after the dropping of atomic bombs on Hiroshima and Nagasaki in 1945 that the public became anxious about radiation, its fears inflamed not only by what actually happened to the survivors of Hiroshima but by the spate of "mutant monster" movies in the 1950s. And it was not until the 1980s that the dangers of radiation treatment and even of X rays brought about the issuance of government guidelines to limit their use.

Haldane's prediction about radiology shops in every neighborhood was thus undermined less by any awareness of detrimental side-effects—which did not really come into play until decades later—as by the fact that scientists were unable to find ways to develop the "combinations of rays" with broader applications than those that already existed when he wrote his essay.

1928 ▶ The existence of anti-matter

Paul A. M. Dirac

In 1928, in England, Paul A. M. Dirac went beyond Einstein to work out an equation that took into account the symmetries involved in the relationship of special relativity and quantum mechanics, building on Einstein's separate theories of 1905. He was horrified to discover that this equation demanded the recognition of a positively charged electron—in other words, the existence of anti-matter. Electrons, which make up matter, carry a negative charge. Like Einstein, who never accepted some of the stranger implications of the quantum mechanics he had first postulated, Dirac was deeply distressed by the discovery of something that seemed to violate perceived reality. But another mathematician, Herman Weyl of Germany, soon showed that either Dirac's basic theory was nonsense or that anti-matter did indeed have to exist. Carl D. Anderson, using the cloud chamber at the California University of Technology, then isolated the positively charged electron in 1932. It was dubbed the positron. When electrons and positrons, matter and anti-matter, encounter each other, they produce energy in the process of mutual annihilation.

Dirac was awarded the Nobel Prize in Physics in 1933, and Anderson received the same award in 1936. Dirac's theoretical identification of the existence of anti-matter and Anderson's confirmation of it in the cloud chamber at Cal Tech formed an essential basis to the enormous development of quantum physics during the remainder of the twentieth century, but quantum physics are so bizarre, and so at odds with the nature of ordinarily observable reality that they sometimes boggle the minds of the scientists who work in the field to this day. It is hardly surprising, in retrospect, that Paul Dirac initially refused to believe the results of his own genius.

1928 No future in movies for Fred Astaire

unnamed MGM executive

No one really knows what makes someone a movie star. It's not just looks; many beautiful people have disappeared after a couple of films. And it's not just acting ability. A number of major stars have limited acting talent, and some of Broadway's greats have failed on the silver screen. So it shouldn't be too surprising that Hollywood executives have often been wrong about the potential of men and women who would become icons of film history. Marilyn Monroe was told to get lost several times. It took Harrison Ford a dozen years to make an impact. But the most famous story about negative responses to a future legend revolves around Fed Astaire.

Like Henry Fonda and Marlon Brando, Fred Astaire was originally from Omaha, Nebraska. Why Omaha should have produced three such very different screen immortals is a mystery in itself. All three first had success on Broadway, Fonda in secondary roles and Brando with an incandescent performance in *A Streetcar Named Desire*, but Fred Astaire had been a Broadway star for a decade when he had his first screen test in 1928. Starting in 1917, he and his sister Adele were among the top Broadway attractions, their two greatest hits being 1924's *Lady Be Good* and 1927's *Funny Face*, both the work of George and Ira Gershwin. But there was no need for musical stars in silent films, and it wasn't until 1927 and the success of the first talking picture, *The Jazz Singer* with Al Jolson, that Hollywood took an interest. Astaire's first screen test led nowhere. After looking at it, an executive at MGM supposedly wrote a memo that said, "Can't act. Can't sing. Balding. Can dance a little."

"Supposedly" is the operative word here. Some experts claim that the reason the MGM executive in unnamed is that no such memo ever existed, but was made up years later. Others think it may well be a genuine quote, since Astaire would meet with similar resistance years later. At any rate, in 1927, no offer was forthcoming from Hollywood, and Astaire went back to Broadway. The hits continued, and his dancing was already being admired by great figures in the world of classical ballet like Serge Diaghilev of the Ballets Russe de Monte Carlo, as it would be later by George Balanchine and Mikhail Baryshnikov. Over the next three years, Fred and Adele took three of their own shows to London after their Broadway runs, and there Adele became engaged to Charles Cavendish, the second son of the Duke of Devonshire. With Adele's marriage in 1932, Fred Astaire was on his own. After a year on Broadway starring in *Gay Divorcee*, and two days after his marriage to Boston socialite Phyllis Potter, he left for Hollywood. Hollywood moguls still had their doubts. They didn't much like his singing, never mind that balding look, and even his dancing remained suspect. Another MGM man, this time named, associate producer Johnny Considine, wrote a memo saying, "You can get dancers like this for $75 a week." Even so, MGM gave him his first movie job, on loan from RKO, where he had signed. It was only a bit, but he got a chance to do a few steps with Joan Crawford in *Dancing Lady*. Then RKO put him in a frothy trifle called *Flying Down to Rio*. He got fifth billing, but he was teamed with Ginger Rogers, the movie was a hit, audiences loved Fred and Ginger, and the rest was history. Not only could he dance a little, he became the by-word in Hollywood elegance. And that slightly reedy voice, as Broadway had known for many years, could do more with a Gershwin song than anyone else ever has.

1929 America couldn't be run without Prohibition

Henry Ford

The Temperance Movement had been in full cry about the evils of drink for seventy years when the 18th Amendment to the Constitution was finally passed in 1917. In the intervening years, state after state, particularly those with large rural populations, had gone "dry." Yet the resistance to Prohibition was so strong in the more cosmopolitan states that it took another two years for the amendment to be ratified by the required two-thirds majority. Ratification took place on January 29, 1919, and Congress then passed a measure to implement the amendment, the Volstead Act. That was challenged in the Supreme Court, which upheld the act on January 5, 1920, and Prohibition officially went into effect on January 16,

1920. The 18th Amendment had prohibited the sale, manufacture, or transportation of alcohol, leading some citizens who got hauled into court to point out that it didn't say anything about not *drinking* liquor, but few judges paid any attention to that technicality.

Nevertheless, Prohibition was in trouble almost from the start. All the major cities had speakeasies, bars disguised as something else, in large numbers. Homemade bathtub gin was making people drunker than ever because of its very high alcohol content, and rural stills were far too numerous to be kept up with by the "revenue man," the agents of the Federal Treasury who were supposed to put them out of business. An entirely new class of criminals developed, specialists in the smuggling and distribution of liquor, and plenty of supposedly respectable businessmen, like Joseph P. Kennedy, later U.S. ambassador to England and father of a future President, amassed fortunes as bootleggers. Thus while drinking proceeded apace, the U.S. Treasury was being deprived of the taxes that had once flowed along with the liquor, with the bootleggers collecting their own forms of "tax," enforced by beatings and murder. Corruption was rampant, with the police and judges being bribed to look the other way.

The worst problem was enforcing the law—Congress never appropriated anything approaching the amount of money needed to do the job. The enforcement tab kept going up, starting at $2.4 million, rising to almost $7 million, then $10 million, with no end in sight. In 1929, the same year that Henry Ford said the country couldn't be run without Prohibition, the commissioner for prohibition, James M. Doran, said it would take $300 million to make enforcement work, but had less than a tenth of that to work with. Senators and Representatives from rural states went right on saying that Prohibition was necessary and would never be repealed. Business leaders like

Henry Ford were convinced that legal drinking would bring on a collapse of industry, with drunken workers bringing assembly lines to a screeching halt. Ford claimed that the need for Prohibition to continue was "an industrial fact."

But other industrialists, including Pierre Dupont, an initial backer, changed their minds. Prohibition was clearly doing more harm than good. More and more voices sided with repeal. In 1932, Franklin Roosevelt ran on a repeal platform—although that was a fairly minor issue in that watershed election. But the Democratic Congress swept into office with him made repeal a priority. The 21st Amendment, nullifying the 18th, was passed on December 5, 1933. Its ratification proceeded with amazing speed. The necessary thirty-sixth state vote to ratify repeal came on April 10, 1934, cast by, of all places, Utah, home to the teetotaling Mormons. Henry Ford was soon proved completely wrong; the assembly lines continued to run like clockwork.

A few states retained their "dry" status for many years. North Carolina was essentially dry into the 1980s. You could bring your own bottle to a restaurant, but the establishment itself couldn't serve anything but beer and wine. Even after the state went "wet," the county surrounding Charlotte remained dry, a fact that local businessmen said had allowed Atlanta instead of Charlotte to become the leader of the New South, and in the early 1990s even Charlotte capitulated to the "demon rum."

1929 ▶ Stocks have reached a permanently high plateau

Irving Fisher

As the Roaring Twenties drew to a close, America was brimming with confidence. Prohibition was still in force despite the prevalence of speakeasies and bathtub gin. The country had survived the Charleston and the short skirts that went with it. Three Republican presidents, Harding, Coolidge, and Hoover, had been elected since women had gotten the vote in 1920, proving to the likes of Sinclair Lewis's fictional Babbitt that even the ladies could be relied upon to uphold Main Street values. And the stock market was at an all-time high, after climbing steadily for years. One Wall Street high roller, John J. Raskob, was even moved to write an article for the *Ladies' Home Journal* called "Everybody Ought to be Rich," advising an investment of $15 a month in stocks. True, in late September, the stock market slipped a bit, but not enough to worry anybody. In fact, on October 17, the esteemed Yale professor of economics Irving Fisher asserted, "Stocks have reached what looks like a permanently high plateau."

But a week later, on October 24, the market took a frightening dive. Despite reassuring statements from many of the country's most important politicians and businessmen, and in total disregard of the fortunes pumped into stocks over the next few days by financiers like J. P. Morgan in an attempt to shore things up, the stock market collapsed, on October 29, and the Great Depression began. The crash didn't really bottom out until March 1933, when the new President, Franklin Delano Roosevelt, took the drastic step of closing the banks temporarily. By then stocks had fallen 80 percent since the "permanently high plateau" of 1929.

Roosevelt got a slew of new controls enacted into law, and greatly increased the power of the Federal Reserve. In recent years still more controls have been implemented to deal with the impact of massive computer transactions, making it possible to shut down the stock exchange on a moment's notice if matters seem to be getting out of hand. This mechanism is based on the assumption that given an overnight respite, investors will get a grip on any incipient panic—the same idea that lay behind Roosevelt's "Bank Holiday." And the fact that 1987's Black Monday was not only weathered but opened the way to the astonishing rise of stock prices in the 1990s also lessened fears of another great crash. These days, in fact, many experts are not content with predicting a high plateau; they believe that there will be a "corrective downswing," but that stocks will then start climbing again. The head of the Federal Reserve, Alan Greenspan, keeps murmuring that stocks may be overvalued, but there are still those willing to predict that the Dow Jones industrial average will break the 10,000 barrier by the year 2000. Nevertheless, the names of John J. Raskob and Irving Fisher should perhaps be recalled from time to time.

1929 Medical potential of penicillin

Alexander Fleming

The history of science overflows with examples of great discoveries flowing from chance events, from the displacement effect in Archimedes' bathwater, through Newton's apple to James Watson's shared office providing a vital link in the discovery of the structure of DNA. Royston M. Roberts has written an entire book on the subject, called *Serendipity—Accidental Discoveries in Science*. But, as many science historians have noted, few of these chains of chance are as astonishing as the one associated with Alexander Fleming's discovery of the wonder drug penicillin. There are so many crucial accidents of time and place in Fleming's story that only a lengthy biographical essay can take them all into account. By example, suffice it to say that the mold he found growing on an uncovered petri dish in his laboratory at St. Mary's Hospital at the University of London seems to have arrived there because a spore from the laboratory on the floor below blew out the window, wafted up one floor, and blew in his window. This required two uncovered petri dishes and two open windows, quite aside from the fact that he was a professor at St. Mary's because he had chosen to attend medical school there for the casual reason that he had played water polo as a teenager against a team from the hospital!

Fleming was an extremely affable, much-liked man, and he did not fit the stereotype of the obsessed scientist at all. He did not work late into the night, his laboratory tended to be something of a mess, and he did not take himself too seriously. It was, of course, his tendency toward lax housekeeping that allowed the mold spore to show up in the first place. But Fleming also had enormous curiosity and was an exceptionally observant man. He not only noticed the clear area around the mold, but wondered what it was. As he himself later noted, many other bacteriologists must have seen a similar mold and simply thrown it out. Instead, he analyzed it. He had done this seven years before when he had had a bad cold, prepared a culture from his own nasal discharge and left it overnight. He was aware that a tear from his own eye, also a result of his cold, had fallen into the culture. When he noticed a clear area surrounding that spot the next day, he investigated and discovered a mild antiseptic that he named *lyzozyme*.

Lysozyme did not prove to have much practical use, and it looked at first that penicillin would not, either. While it proved to be harmless to body cells and had no toxic effects when injected into animals, Fleming was unable to produce penicillin in sufficiently concentrated doses to tell whether it would be a truly effective antibiotic. It was simply too unstable to survive in a solution of the amplitude necessary for further tests. Then in the late 1930s, the Australian-born bacteriologist Howard Florey began working with the young German refugee Ernst Chain, testing Fleming's lyzozyme and penicillin, along with other natural antibiotics, in laboratories at Oxford University. New techniques, including freeze-drying, now made it possible to produce penicillin in sufficient concentrations to carry out tests on mice and then human beings, which demonstrated the drug's extraordinary ability to kill staphylococcal bacteria. A crash program, much of it carried out at the U.S. Department of Agriculture laboratory in Peoria, Illinois, produced enough penicillin to save thousands of lives during the Second World War—large numbers of soldiers in the First World War had died not from their wounds, but from infections that took hold in them.

The question of who should get credit for this new wonder drug arose. Should it be Fleming, who first discovered it, or Florey and Chain, who worked out how to use it. Since Fleming had written a report in 1929 that stated, "It is suggested that it may be an efficient antiseptic for application to, or injection into, areas infected with penicillin-sensitive microbes," his own claim was clear. Fleming had not only discovered penicillin but predicted the use that Florey and Chain had made possible. In the scientific community, all three men were seen as sharing the glory, as they did when they were named recipients of the Nobel Prize in Physiology or Medicine for 1945. But as far as the press was concerned, the affable Fleming was the real hero, and it is his name that has become indelibly associated with penicillin in the public mind. Fleming was somewhat embarrassed by this turn of events, but in many ways it seems a fitting capstone to the extraordinary chain of accidents and luck that allowed this particular man to make one of the most useful discoveries in the history of medicine.

1931 ▶ The existence of neutrinos

Wolfgang Pauli

As physicists learned more and more about the subatomic world in the 1920s, they encountered a problem. In that strange new world, something was missing. As George Gamow explained in his famous 1947 book, *One, Two, Three . . . Infinity*, "The missing thing was energy, and since energy, according to one of the oldest and most stable laws of physics, can be neither created nor destroyed, the discovery that energy that should have been present was absent indicated that there must have been a thief, or gang of thieves, that took it away."

In 1931, the great Austrian physicist, Wolfgang Pauli, who later fled Hitler to the United States, came up with an answer to the problem. He hypothesized that the gang of thieves were what came to be called "neutrinos," elementary particles that carried no charge and so little mass that they could pass through matter, including human beings, by the billions completely unnoticed. The only clue they left behind was the energy they stole away with them. Mathematically, this solution stood up, and it worked so well that by the time Gamow wrote his book, neutrinos were almost universally accepted by physicists as a crucial element in the subatomic universe. Nevertheless, their existence had not been demonstrated in any physical experiment.

It took until 1956 for empirical evidence of the existence of the neutrino to be provided. It was done by the American physicists Clyde L. Cowan, Jr., and Frederick Reins, who used a nuclear fission reactor for their experiments. They succeeded in detecting the presence of antineutrinos, which was as good as finding the neutrinos themselves, since in the subatomic world the existence of an anti-particle demands the existence of its opposite. Wolfgang Pauli, who won the Nobel Prize in Physics for 1945, had indeed fingered the correct gang of thieves a quarter century earlier.

1933 ▸ Impossibility of utilizing atomic energy

Ernest Rutherford

In 1901, Ernest Rutherford and Frederick Soddy discovered the nature of radiation, the fact that atoms gave off energy when they changed form. By 1933, Rutherford, who had won the Nobel Prize in Chemistry in 1908, had become Lord Rutherford and was the grand old man of British science. But although a great deal more had been discovered about atoms in the intervening decades, little progress had been made in harnessing the energy released by atoms. Perhaps because of the creeping conservatism that affects even great scientific minds as they age, and probably also out of frustration, Rutherford told the *New York Times*, "Anyone who says that . . . with our present knowledge we can utilize atomic energy is talking moonshine." Speaking for the record, he had hedged by using the phrase "with our present knowledge," but privately he even used the word "never" to describe the possibility of putting atomic energy to useful work.

One of those who was provoked by Rutherford's use of the word "never" was a young colleague named Leo Szilard, who had recently fled Hitler's Germany and was working in a laboratory at St. Bart's Hospital in London. One morning, while walking from the Strand Hotel, where he lived (Szilard loved hotels, and lived in one while working on the Manhattan Project in America a decade later), he had to pause for a red light near St. Bart's. By the time the light changed, he had come up with an answer to Rutherford's "never." He realized that if an atom was hit by one neutron with sufficient force to break up the atom and release two neutrons, you would have what he immediately began calling a chain reaction. Szilard filed a patent on this idea in 1934, which eventually led him to the University of Chicago as a leader of the Manhattan Project. It was there, working with Enrico Fermi and others, that Szilard was to see his London street-corner inspiration reach fruition with the success of the first controlled nuclear chain reaction.

There is a lesson here. For the sake of his own reputation, no grand old man of science should ever say "never" in the presence of a younger colleague. On the other hand, great scientists like Rutherford keep doing just that, with the result that their cheeky young colleagues, like Leo Szilard, decide to prove them wrong, to the eternal benefit of scientific inquiry.

1933 ▸ The rising of Atlantis

Edgar Cayce

The American healer and prophet Edgar Cayce, who lived from 1877 to 1945, had a considerable following in his lifetime, which continues to this day in some quarters. Although not an M.D., he had an uncanny diagnostic ability, and was brought in as an advisor by several physicians on difficult cases. His ideas about how to achieve and maintain physical well-being, and how physical well-being tied in with mental attitude, have found their way into present day "holistic" medicine and various New Age beliefs. His diagnostic expertise was well-documented, but because he was also known for his prophecies, most of which were based on knowledge that he said came to him during trancelike periods of sleep, he was inevitably called a "quack" by the guardians of traditional medical practice.

Like most prophets, he was vague about specific dates, and adept at using language that gave him a great deal of leeway in claiming accuracy. Earthquakes, floods, and wars were his prophetic territory. Among many other things, he predicted that part of California would fall into the sea, a notion that many seismologists would agree is not only possible but quite likely. The question is: when? Cayce said it would happen, along with many other events he predicted, sometime between 1958 and 1998. Unless an extraordinary number of catastrophes occur around the world during 1997, his time will have run out on most of the predictions he made.

Cayce's most famous prediction concerned the rising of the lost continent of Atlantis from the sea. Like many others interested in the story of Atlantis, originally set down by Plato but even then treated as a "legend," Cayce believed that the continent had existed in the Atlantic between the Caribbean islands and the Azores, which were regarded as remnants of Atlantis. For some reason, Cayce was somewhat more specific on the timing of the rise of Atlantis than was the case with most of his prophecies. Jess Stern, who wrote a best-selling book on Cayce called *The Sleeping Prophet*, published in 1967, pieced together Cayce's various pronouncements on the subject to pinpoint the anticipated reappearance of a large chunk of Atlantis in 1968 or 1969. (This bit of timing in no way hurt sales of Stern's book.) It was to occur somewhere in the Caribbean. Atlantis, of course, did not rise to the bait, which may have disappointed millions of tabloid readers around the world, but no doubt came as a relief to inhabitants of the Caribbean.

▶ 1934   The existence of the "quark"

James Joyce

This entry is in one sense a joke. But it also underscores an important point.

Quantum physics, whose foundations were laid by Einstein in 1905, have replaced Newton's laws as the focal point of twentieth-century scientific inquiry. These investigations into the subatomic particles that make up the universe have led to insights so peculiar, from the proven existence of stellar black holes to the theoretical possibility of alternate universes, that they sometimes seem to go beyond the wildest imaginings of science fiction. Much of quantum physics remains a matter of theory, but more than enough of its strange reality has been demonstrated by empirical experiment to prove its fundamental importance to the nature of the universe.

Quantum physics identifies two general categories of subatomic particles, one of which, fermions, form all matter, while the other, bosons, convey force. Fermions, named after the Nobel physicist Enrico Fermi, one of the reluctant fathers of the atomic bomb, can be further divided into large numbers of particles (too many, in the view of some physicists), which, despite their annoying variety, can be generally classified as either quarks or leptons.

Quarks were the brainchild of the Cal Tech physicist Murray Gell-Mann. Gell-Mann was a man of enormous erudition in a great many fields, a rival of Richard Feynman for the title of "world's smartest man." Gell-Mann was an expert on James Joyce, among his many other accomplishments, and he decided to name the new particle he had envisioned after a word that appears in Joyce's notoriously difficult novel *Finnegans Wake.* There, Joyce had written the sentence, "Three quarks for Muster Mark!" Quark is only one of thousands of made-up words in the novel, and Gell-Mann could easily have chosen many others. But it is worth noting that the word *quark* rhymes with the name of the imaginary creature in Lewis Carroll's famous nonsense poem "The Hunting of the Snark." Carroll, who was a mathematician of some note himself, is a favorite writer among theoretical physicists because his topsy-turvy worlds, on the other side of the looking glass, have a strange logic that reminds quantum physicists of their own unseen realms. Carroll's snark is as elusive a creature as Gell-Mann's quark, something that must be there but doesn't want to be seen, let alone caught.

Gell-Mann's choice of a name for his particle exhibits the sense of humor that is common among advanced physicists. But it is also a reminder—and here is the important point—that great scientists throughout history have seen themselves not as the cold, dry calculating sorts that popular prejudice would have them be, but rather as men of imagination, even as artists of a kind. From Aristotle down through Copernicus, Galileo, Newton, Einstein, and Gell-Mann to the present day, the greatest minds trying to make sense of the physical universe have talked about the *beauty* of their equations. They look for *harmonies;* indeed, they have often been so seduced by the beauty of certain ideas that false concepts such as the Aristotelian view of the Earth as the center of the universe can endure for centuries.

Quantum physicists are obsessed with the goal of producing a "unified theory" of the universe that will tie together the peculiarities of subatomic particles and the everyday Newtonian laws of physics, particularly in respect to gravity, in a form that attains a transcendent and beautiful harmony. Thus it is only fitting that Murray Gell-Mann should take the name of his extraordinary particle from the work of a great writer, and in the process turn James Joyce into a predictor of deeper mysteries than he knew.

1936 ▶ Alf Landon will be elected president

William Randolph Hearst

William Randolph Hearst, the model for Orson Welles's *Citizen Kane*, was the most powerful media mogul of his time. His tabloid-style newspapers, including one in almost every major American city, were run with an iron hand—they were told not to review or even accept ads for *Citizen Kane*, for example. Hearst loathed Franklin Delano Roosevelt with such passion that he managed to convince himself that Alf Landon, the Kansas governor nominated by the Republicans for president in 1936, was going to oust F.D.R. from the White House after one term, and save the country from the "socialist" ideas he was using to combat the Great Depression. In an August 1936 editorial, following Landon's nomination, Hearst wrote, "The race will not be close at all. Landon will be overwhelmingly elected and I'll stake my reputation as a prophet on it."

Hearst lost his stake, big time. Roosevelt was elected to a second term by an electoral margin of 523 to 8, with Landon carrying only Maine and Vermont. In the popular vote, Roosevelt outpolled Landon by 11 million votes out of 40 million cast. It remains the most lopsided victory in the history of presidential politics; even Walter Mondale's 1984 loss to Ronald Reagan wasn't as bad in terms of the popular vote, although Mondale carried only Washington, D.C., and his home state of Minnesota. Landon, a genial man, took his loss with good grace, and lived to see his daughter, Nancy Kassebaum, become a distinguished Republican senator from Kansas. A conservative with a moderate streak, much like her father, she retired in 1996 after serving three terms in the Senate.

1938 ▶ The imminent discovery of atomic power

John W. Campbell

By 1938 it had been thirty-seven years since Ernest Rutherford and Frederick Soddy had discovered that radiation involved the changing of one kind of atom into another, and the radiation itself showing that energy was being released. For the following quarter century, there was great speculation, by scientists, journalists, and science-fiction writers, about when and how this vast energy source might be harnessed. Innumerable utopian dreams featured the use of atomic power. But no answers were forthcoming from the laboratories of the world's foremost physicists as to how atomic energy could be released in sufficient quantities to be useful or how such energy might be controlled if it were released. The dean of American physicists, Robert Millikan, stated in 1930 that solar energy was a more likely source of future power than atomic energy. And Ernest Rutherford told *The New York Times* in September 1933: "Anyone who says that . . . with our present knowledge we can utilize atomic energy is talking moonshine."

But there remained some true believers. One of them was John W. Campbell, the young editor of *Astounding*

Science Fiction. When he took over the magazine in 1935, it was strictly a pulp magazine, full of space battles against BEMs (Bug-Eyed Monsters), but he quickly moved to make it more scientifically respectable, and drew an increasingly educated audience. Many men who would go on to become astronomers, physicists, NASA engineers, and science writers were inspired by *Astounding* in their youth. Campbell had a background in atomic physics himself, and he was certain that an atomic age was coming. In June 1938, his monthly editorial proclaimed, *"The discoverer of the secret of atomic power is alive on Earth today.* His papers and research are appearing regularly; his name is known." Of course, Campbell did not know the exact identity of that discoverer, just that the person had to exist.

Six months later, just before Christmas, a group of European physicists succeeded in splitting the uranium atom. Otto Robert Frisch, one of the group, took note that what happened resembled the dividing of a biological cell, and asked a friend who was a biologist what that process was called. The answer was fission. In his book *Nuclear Fear,* Spencer R. Weart tells what happened next: "Frisch explained uranium fission to the director of his institute, Niels Bohr, who was just then departing for the United States. In January 1939 Bohr told a meeting of American physicists about the discovery, and one of the science reporters who tended to hover around such meetings immediately put fission into the newspapers. Journalists and scientists everywhere were caught up in the excitement, and through 1939 they wrote hundreds of articles to inform people around the world."

And John W. Campbell was able to say, "I told you so," in his editorial of April 1939. The problem of harnessing atomic fission remained to be found, but the secret of releasing it had been at last revealed.

1938 ▸ "Peace in our time"

Neville Chamberlain

Born in 1869, Neville Chamberlain came from a wealthy and distinguished family, but had made his own mark by the time he was forty, profiting from the metal-working industry in Birmingham, England. He was chosen to serve as Lord Mayor of that city in 1915, organized England's first municipal bank in 1916, and made a start in national politics as head of national service in David Lloyd George's coalition World War I government. First elected to the House of Commons in 1918, Chamberlain had a typical rise through the ranks of the Conservative party, holding a variety of government posts, including two stints as Chancellor of the Exchequer. He had served in that position for six straight years when he became prime minister on May 29, 1937.

As prime minister he desperately tried to avoid having Britain dragged into a European war, but his policies were tarred with the name of "appeasement." In April 1938 he recognized Italy's seizure of Ethiopia, attempting to keep Mussolini from getting too close to Hitler, a plan that did not work. He did keep Great Britain out of the Spanish Civil War, to the outrage of some and the relief of many. But in 1938 he also made three trips to Germany to try to deal with Hitler's demand that Czechoslovakia cede the Sudetenland to Germany. This led to selling out Czechoslovakia entirely in the Munich Agreement of September 30, 1938, which he and France's premier, Edouard Daladier, signed with Hitler. This was initially a popular move in Great Britain, as Chamberlain proclaimed that he had achieved "peace in our time." Despite this wildly optimistic prediction, Chamberlain was no fool: he also stepped up the rate of Britain's rearmament. When Hitler annexed the rest of Czechoslovakia in less than six months, Chamberlain had to repudiate the Munich Agreement. The British and French then guaranteed armed support for Poland, Rumania, and Greece if Hitler should invade them, and subsequently made a more specific pact with Poland. Hitler's invasion of that country led to a British declaration of war on September 3, 1939. Presiding over the early stages of World War II, he brought Winston Churchill, the member of his own party who had most severely attacked the Munich Agreement, into his cabinet. On the day of Germany's invasion of the Low Countries, May 10, 1939, Chamberlain resigned. Churchill became prime minister as head of a coalition government, and called on Chamberlain to serve as Lord President of the Council, but within months he had to resign because of his health and died a few weeks later on November 9, 1940.

Chamberlain's "peace in our time" prediction, and his general appeasement of the fascists, led to his being held in contempt for decades, even as his old rival Churchill was elevated to the pantheon of history's great leaders. But there has been a reappraisal in recent years, with greater emphasis placed on his ongoing preparations for war despite his attempts to maintain peace. It is now felt that his prediction of peace was more a matter of hope than belief.

1938 ► No attack on Pearl Harbor

George Fielding Eliot

A former diplomat named George Fielding Eliot wrote an article in 1938 for the prestigious *American Mercury* in which he heaped scorn on the idea that the United States needed to worry about war with Japan as well as Hitler's European ambitions. "A Japanese attack on Pearl Harbor," he wrote, "is a practical impossibility." He was hardly alone in this assessment. Voices warning about Japan's expansionist adventures in Asia tended to get short shrift during that period. The isolationist idea that had taken hold in America following World War I were still in vogue twenty years later. Americans didn't even want to hear about joining Great Britain and France against Hitler in what seemed an inevitable European war, never mind think about Japan.

More prescient views had existed earlier in the century, however. As Alvin Toffler points out in *Previews and Premises*, as far back as 1908, the influential if "proto-fascist" Homer Lea had predicted that war with Japan was inevitable. Lea believed that economic rivalry would lead the United States into conflict with Japan, and that "yellow peril" racism in America would heighten the tensions. By 1931, with Japan's invasion of Manchuria, it became clear that the Empire of the Rising Sun had long-range plans for the domination of the Far East. The United States had maintained an "Open Door Policy" with Japan since 1899, and some compromises had been made on both sides to keep the relationship on an even keel. Although that was still the case when Eliot wrote his *American Mercury* article in 1938, the very fact that he needed to proclaim the safety of Pearl Harbor indicated a nervous awareness of the hard-line faction that was rising to power in Japan. By 1940, Japanese militarists had taken over the government. Having already established themselves along the coast of China, the Japanese seized French Indochina in 1940 with the blessing of their Axis allies, Germany and Italy. That act threatened the whole continent, from the Dutch East Indies, with its huge oil reserves, through the British-dominated Malay Peninsula, to India itself. Washington, of course, was particularly concerned about its bases in the Philippines. By late 1941, the U.S. Secretary of War Henry L. Stimson said that the real question about the Japanese was "how we should maneuver them into the position of firing the first shot." The Roosevelt Administration had done all that it could to aid Great Britain in secondary ways against Hitler. War with Japan would inevitably also mean war against Japan's ally Germany. Why then, with tensions building acutely, was the December 7, 1941, attack on Pearl Harbor such a surprise?

This is a question that historians have never been able to adequately answer. At the time, there was a faction, of which George Field Eliot was representative, that thought that Japan wouldn't dare attack the United States or its possessions, and that an attack on Pearl Harbor was a military impossibility. This group later charged that Roosevelt had, in fact, made U.S. forces in the Pacific a sitting target in order to get into the war despite public resistance at home. But, in fact, Washington was certain an attack was coming, sooner rather than later. The American ambassador to Japan, Joseph Grew, had warned of it. The United States had cracked the Japanese code, and knew that current negotiations were essentially meaningless. It was not known where an attack would come, or exactly when, although most American military leaders believed it would be on the Philippine bases. The American commanders both there and in Hawaii were sent warning cables from Washington. The U.S. Army and Navy commanders in Hawaii decided against putting their forces on constant alert for an attack that might still be days or weeks away. The warning from Washington may not have been strong enough, although it seems clear enough; it began with the words, "This dispatch is to be considered a war warning," and was followed by another message on December 6 that included the words, "Hostilities may ensue." Following the devastating attack on December 7, both commanders at Pearl Harbor—General Walter C. Short and Admiral Husband E. Kimmel—were forced to resign in disgrace.

For the United States, the December 7, 1941, attack on Pearl Harbor was, in President Roosevelt's words, "a day that will live in infamy." But, on the other side of the Atlantic, Prime Minister Winston Churchill reacted to the news of the attack with the words, "Thanks be to God. We are saved." That prediction was absolutely correct.

1938 ► Cloning

Hans Spemann

The first suggestion of what would come to be called cloning came from Dr. Hans Spemann of Germany in 1938. Considered the first modern embryologist, Spemann came up with the idea of removing the nucleus from an egg cell and substituting the nucleus of another cell. Even Spemann called this a "fantastical experiment," and no one had any idea how to do it; in fact no one at the time even knew what genetic material was composed of or the nature of its structure. Experiments on frogs, which have extremely large eggs, began in the early 1950s, but it was to be twenty years until John Gurdon of Great Britain succeeded at that task. But over many years, the resulting spawn never lived beyond the tadpole stage. And these were frogs—almost no one believed the procedure could be carried out with mammals. The entire field was nearly dealt a death blow in 1983, when it was discovered that an apparently successful cloning of the embryo cells of mice carried out two years earlier had been faked. Many scientists got out of that field of research altogether, and those who remained were often subjected to the only slightly veiled scorn of their colleagues.

One who did not give up was Dr. Ian Wilmut, who had worked quietly at the Roslin Institute in Edinburgh, Scotland, for twenty-three years when he finally met with success at the age of 52. The announcement on February 22, 1997, that he and his colleagues had succeeded in cloning an adult sheep brought banner headlines around the world. He had taken DNA from the mammary cell of an adult sheep and fused it with the unfertilized egg of another sheep, after first removing the DNA from the nucleus of that egg. The resulting embryo was then transferred to still another sheep that acted as a surrogate mother. The cloned lamb, with exactly the same genetic makeup as the original adult, was born in July 1996, and called Dolly. At the age of seven months, Dolly was apparently healthy and normal.

Dr. Wilmut's utterly unexpected announcement created many different kinds of shock waves. Scientists who thought it couldn't be done were confounded. Several prominent geneticists ruefully noted that the funding necessary to carry out such an experiment would not have been available to mainstream genetic laboratories, particularly in America, both because such research was considered a dead end and because it had developed a some-what disreputable aura due to the hoax exposed in 1983. Because Dr. Wilmut and his colleagues were working in the field of animal husbandry, they were able both to get funding and to work undisturbed. Dr. Wilmut's primary purpose in pursuing cloning was to facilitate the production of animals whose protein could be used to develop drugs to combat human diseases.

But experts on medical ethics, religious leaders, politicians, and newspaper editorials immediately began worrying about the sudden possibility that human beings might eventually be cloned. Visions of the 1978 movie *The Boys from Brazil,* based on an Ira Levin novel about producing multiple clones from Hitler's DNA, leapt to mind. In several countries, including the United States, high-level government commissions were immediately assembled to study the implications and to make recommendations of laws that ought to be passed to control or ban future cloning efforts. Medical scientists and ethicists worried about the pressure to add cloning to the increasing number of procedures available to infertile couples who want children.

Cooler heads tried to calm things down by noting that plants had been cloned for centuries—taking a cutting from one plant and sticking it in another pot is a form of cloning. The piles of bananas we see in supermarkets are usually genetic clones, the differences between them caused by the fact that some get more sun than others. This point was extended to explain that a clone of a human adult might have the same genetic material but, because the resulting child would grow up in a different time and would have unique experiences, a quite different person would be likely to result.

But this kind of information did not seem to persuade most people to endorse the notion of cloning human beings. An overwhelming majority of those polled on the issue strongly disapproved of the idea of cloning human beings, but most believed that since it was possible, someone would eventually do it.

1939 ▶ The existence of "black holes"

J. Robert Oppenheimer

J. Robert Oppenheimer is best remembered for his role as "the father of the atomic bomb," as head of the Manhattan Project team that devised a way of harnessing atomic fission so that it could be contained in a usable bomb. But even before that, he had published a notable paper on what would happen when stars any larger than twice the size of our sun collapsed into neutron stars. His calculations demonstrated that the collapse of larger stars would continue to the point that they became so small, while retaining such enormous mass, that their gravity would prevent any light (or, indeed, anything at all) from escaping them.

In making this claim, Oppenheimer was expanding on work done eleven years earlier by a young physicist named Subrahmanyan Chanrasekar, who had theorized that stellar cores more than 1.4 times the size of the sun could not become the commonly observed white dwarfs, but would continue to collapse due to their gravity. The Russian physicist, Lev Davidovich Landau, came to a similar conclusion at about the same time in 1928. But most physicists were not ready for this idea. Sir Arthur Eddington, whose measurements during the solar eclipse of 1919 had confirmed Einstein's theory of relativity, was outraged by Chanrasekar's theory. "I think there should be a law of nature to prevent a star from behaving in this absurd way!" he said. Oppenheimer's claim that a star would continue to collapse, if it were somewhat larger, until no light could escape it, was met with almost the same reaction from the American physicist John Archibald Wheeler.

Of course Oppenheimer was eventually proven right, and both Chanrasekar and Landau shared the Nobel Prize for physics in 1983 for their initial work on this subject. Wheeler himself was eventually so completely won over that he gave the name "black holes" to Oppenheimer's stars in 1969. Remarkably, two years earlier, "Star Trek" had made reference to one of these collapsed stars in an early episode of the series. In *The Physics of Star Trek*, Lawrence M. Krauss writes, "When I watched this episode early in the preparation of this book, I found it amusing that 'Star Trek' writers had gotten the name wrong. Now I realize that they very nearly invented it!" But it was J. Robert Oppenheimer who conceived of these stellar peculiarities.

1939 The perfect city surrounded by perfect suburbs

Henry Dreyfuss

The 1939 New York World's Fair—like all World's Fairs—was about optimism. But this one, which took place as Hitler was annexing Europe, outdid them all in predicting peace and prosperity. One of its centerpieces was a futuristic model city, called Democracity, designed by Henry Dreyfuss. Its most unrealistic aspect was the virtual elimination of a police force, deemed unnecessary because there were no slums to breed crime. Poverty had been banished from Democracity—no one said to where. But it promulgated another idea that seemed so attainable to so many important people that it would change the face of America in the years following World War II. This was the idea that an improved city was consistent with the development of large suburbs around it. The city itself was somehow supposed to become a central business hub—clean, uncongested, and with ample parking, to which the people in those suburbs would travel easily on a daily basis to work, shop, and be entertained.

It was no accident that this idea should have its genesis at the 1939 World's Fair. One of its chief planners was Robert Moses, a man with highways and suburbs on the brain. Rising to a position of power in the postwar years that in many ways exceeded that of the various governors of New York State, he was responsible for the building of the Long Island Expressway, which would come to be known as "the longest parking lot in the world." The flight to the safe, new, clean suburbs would serve to erode the tax base of New York City and other major metropolises across the country, bring us the mall and its seedy cousin, the strip mall, create endless traffic jams both within and without the city, and spew enough exhaust fumes to make air pollution a national crisis.

Of course Robert Moses wasn't the only villain, nor the first. The oil magnates who bribed and strong-armed the city officials of Los Angeles to tear up its model trolley system in the 1930s, so that everyone would have to use cars and buy the gasoline to put into them, were there before him. Businessmen with similar ideas cropped up all across the country. Few of them recognized what their plans would do to America's great cities, and it is doubtful that they would have cared. By the time they were through, the promised land of the suburbs found itself saddled with problems of crime and drug use that had supposedly been left behind in the cities. The cities, on the other hand, teetered for years on the edge of collapse. But then some of them—Pittsburgh, Boston, Baltimore—began remaking themselves, so that by the mid-1990s something of a happy ending was beginning to take shape. While still coping with poverty and crime, many cities are now attracting people back from the suburbs. But there is still no sign of anything like Henry Dreyfuss's Democracity. There are planned communities, a few of them, around the United States, that have achieved a good deal of the felicity promised at the 1939 World's Fair. But there is something they all have in common that was not a part of that imagined future. They're all small towns, not cities.

1939 ▸ Television will elevate dramatic tastes

David Sarnoff

In 1939, the General Electric company and its RCA subsidiary were ready to introduce commercial television on a widespread basis. The real push for the new medium was then delayed until after World War II because the factories that would have manufactured the new sets were needed to produce military technology. But as the 1939 public relations onslaught for the new medium was starting, the CEO of RCA, David Sarnoff, confidently predicted, "It is probable that television drama of high caliber and produced by first-rate artists will materially raise the level of dramatic taste of the nation." When television sets did start appearing in households across the nation a decade later, this prediction initially seemed to have at least some hope of coming true. Although the most popular programs, like those of Milton Berle and Red Skelton, were mostly a throwback to vaudeville—a cleaned-up vaudeville—there were a number of programs on the air in the 1950s that did draw on the talents of serious dramatists and top-flight Broadway actors. *Playhouse 90*, *Studio One*, and *Omnibus* brought first-rate dramatic art into millions of homes. But it soon became apparent that they were not being watched by nearly as many people as the sitcoms, westerns and crime dramas that filled most of the television schedule. One by one, the serious programs bit the dust, unable to corral the legions of viewers advertisers demanded.

Television was already being decried as a "wasteland" by the 1960s, accused of lowering rather than elevating public taste. There have always been a few inspired sitcoms on the air, from *I Love Lucy* to *Seinfeld*, as well as dramatic programs that actually succeeded at interweaving social commentary into their plots. There has been room also for the occasional dramatic special that aimed higher, as exemplified by the periodic offerings of *The Hallmark Hall of Fame*. But a great deal of what's on television, at any hour of the day, is second-rate when it isn't outright dreck. That, of course, was the reason for the creation of public television, which has combined government, corporate, and viewer support to present the kind of programming Sarnoff predicted would prevail. But better still doesn't mean better ratings. PBS has always operated by the skin of its financial teeth, and in the 1990s many conservative politicians have been trying to kill its crucial government funding altogether. It is perfectly possible to make a solid case that television, in spite of its many failings, enriches people's lives, but it is far easier to make a case that it distorts the world, erodes intelligence, and warps the minds of children. It has not come to be called "the boob tube" simply because that makes for a cute rhyme.

Sarnoff's prediction may have had an element of hype to begin with, although it's clear from the record that he believed what he was saying. He was at the forefront of a new medium of communication and he wanted to believe that it would not only make him even wealthier but also improve the world. Leaders of revolutions, whether essentially peaceful technological ones, or violent political ones, are always able to persuade themselves that they are ultimately working for the common good. But given Sarnoff's failed prophecy, we might do well to be somewhat skeptical of current predictions by true believers (who also stand to get rich) that the Internet and other aspects of the information highway are going to make the world a much more knowledgeable place. That the information highway will change the world, just as television did, is a safe prediction. That it will improve the world is another matter entirely.

1940 ▸ Moving highways

Robert Heinlein

In one of his earliest short stories, which marked its author from the start as a major new voice in science fiction, Robert Heinlein imagined a technical development that would revolutionize mass transportation. Published in *Astounding Science Fiction* in June 1940, "The Roads Must Roll" tells the story of a wildcat strike by the engineers who keep America's foremost mode of ground transportation running. The "roads" in question are essentially broad conveyor belts running parallel to one another, with each belt traveling at a different speed. The belt closest to a station platform would move at only ten miles an hour, making it possible for a person to step onto it with ease. Each successive belt further out from the station would run ten miles faster, up to speeds of as much as ninety miles an hour. Depending on how far an individual was going, he or she would move belt by belt toward the middle of the highway (there would be belts going the opposite way on the other side of a median).

This idea enthralled science fiction fans—and gave automobile manufacturers the willies. Heinlein's story is set in the 1980s, and obviously he was off the predictive mark. But even at the time, engineers felt that such a transportation system was technically feasible if the necessary resolve and funding were available for such a project. Atomic power, computers, and developments in both metallurgy and plastics would obviously make it much more feasible now. But Heinlein, who was never much interested in psychology, ignored a crucial fact: the American love of the automobile, not least for the freedom to roam at will it allows. Heinlein's roads might well be possible, but they would also require a drastic alteration in the national psyche to make people want them. Indeed, to judge by the number of idiots who stop dead in their tracks to look around the moment they step off a department-store escalator, a change in human nature itself might be required. It is all too easy to imagine people going down like ninepins on Heinlein's roads if one or two people failed to step lively. What's more, such "roads" would put an end to the joys of tailgating, passing a bigger car, and weaving in and out of traffic. Little wonder this particular prediction came acropper.

⊿1941 Plastic car bodies

Yale Scientific Magazine

As noted by Christopher Cerf and Victor Navasky in *The Experts Speak*, the *Yale Scientific Magazine* predicted in 1941 that "next year's cars should be rolling out of Detroit with plastic bodies." This prediction came before the attack on Pearl Harbor that brought the United States into World War II, which curtailed the production of anything but military vehicles until 1946. The first plastic products were the result of an accidental discovery by two New Jersey brothers, John and Isaiah Hyatt, in 1863. They used it to make billiard balls, which were in short supply because of the decline of the African ivory trade. As recounted by Royston M. Roberts in *Serendipity*, this early compound was not too successful for this purpose since the balls had a tendency to explode when they hit one another with sufficient force. But they subsequently patented their discovery as Celluloid, and by the end of the century the material was being used in a wide range of products from dental plates to fountain pens.

The chemical foundations for many other kinds of plastics were discovered in 1877 by the chemists Charles Friedel and James M. Crafts, eventually leading to the development of polymers and styrenes, as well as synthetic rubber. Throughout the decades prior to World War II, more and more varieties of plastic were synthesized, and by 1941 it may have seemed that the more advanced classes of the material would be eminently usable in car bodies—if they were good for radio cabinets and luggage, why not car doors? The problem, of course, was strength. Luggage can get kicked around a lot, and the plastics of which was made were durable enough to take quite a beating and emerge looking better than leather would. But luggage doesn't have to withstand high-speed collisions.

It would take nearly a half century before plastic with tensile strength sufficient to meet federal safety standards was developed. Finally, in 1990, General Motors became the first automobile manufacturer to turn out large numbers of vehicles with all-plastic bodies—20 percent of the cars produced, and 50 percent of the vans. Because there have been plastic products for more than a century, it is easy to forget that its now ubiquitous presence grew incrementally over a long period of time. Few modern inventions have had a greater impact on our lives—but few have taken longer to reach their full potential.

1944 The atom bomb

Cleve Cartmill

Speculative science fiction stories about the potential uses of atomic energy became fairly common in the 1930s, although most were vague about the scientific details and the weapons suggested had no more basis in reality than the ray guns of Saturday morning movie serials for kids. But in 1937, twenty-nine-year-old John W. Campbell, who had a solid background in atomic physics, took over as editor of *Astounding Stories* (which he would subsequently re-name *Astounding Science Fiction*), and a new degree of plausibility was encouraged. Once the Second World War got under way, U.S. military intelligence began to keep track of science-fiction magazines, as well as scientific journals. When a story called "Nerves" by Lester del Rey appeared in 1942, it was immediately put on the classified list at the atomic laboratories in Oak Ridge, Tennessee, even though the story dealt with peaceful industrial uses of atomic energy, and despite the fact that the magazine could be bought at the newsstand in town. (Classified document silliness has a long history.)

Military intelligence received a much greater jolt, however, when Cleve Cartmill's story "Deadline" appeared in *Astounding* in the summer of 1944. It was disturbing in that the fictional scientists were involved in research akin to that being pursued in the actual development of the top-secret atomic bomb. What really blew the minds of security officers was that Cartmill had given the secret government organization in his story the code name "Hudson River Project." This was far too close to the code name for the real entity, the Manhattan Project, to be easily dismissed as coincidence. Military intelligence officers immediately descended on Cartmill and Campbell and questioned them for hours. They were finally convinced that Cartmill had spun his story out of publicly known facts about atomic research in general, and had no access whatsoever to secret information. His uncanny choice of a code name had been perfectly reasonable; like the government, he had tried to come up with a name that sounded like an innocuous public works program.

Still, military intelligence tried to persuade John W. Campbell to stop publishing stories about atomic energy for the duration of the war. Campbell sensibly argued that to suddenly quit publishing stories on such a common science fiction subject would *arouse* suspicion in itself. The absence of such stories would be more glaring than their presence. Reluctantly, military intelligence accepted his view of the situation.

In the annals of fictional predictions of scientific development, none has been closer to the immediate truth than Cartmill's story. His fictional "Deadline" was only months away from being met at White Sands, New Mexico.

1945 ► Communications satellites

Arthur C. Clarke

Arthur C. Clarke is one of the most important science fiction writers of the second half of the twentieth century, renowned for such visionary novels as *Childhood's End* and *Rendezvous with Rama*, and for his script for the 1968 movie *2001: A Space Odyssey*, co-written with director Stanley Kubrick and adapted from his own short story, "Sentinel." But Clarke is the rare science-fiction writer who imagined possible futures while making a major scientific contribution to the world we now live in.

As a child, Clarke's interest in science was so great that he constructed his own telescope and mapped the moon with it. Too poor to go to college, he worked as an auditor for the government from 1936 to 1941, and then joined the Royal Air Force. He worked in the RAF's radar unit, a fast-developing field during World War II. At the same time he published his first science-fiction short stories. In 1945, while still in the RAF, he published a technical scientific article called "Extra-Terrestrial Relays." Not only did this article predict a system of communications satellites that would relay radio and television signals all over the planet, it detailed the best orbit in which to place such satellites. This was a geosynchronous orbit exactly matching the Earth's sidereal day rotation of 23 hours, 59 minutes, and 6 seconds. At the time this article appeared in *Wireless*

World, it was regarded more as fiction than science. Yet only twenty years later, the first Early Bird satellites were put in place in exactly the orbit he had recommended, which has come to be called the Clarke orbit.

Communications satellites are the keystone of what Marshall McLuhan called the "global village." They can bring us nearly instantaneous live television feeds from anywhere in the world and serve an ever-increasing variety of communications needs, including the World Wide Web. In just over thirty years, they have changed the world, and will be integral to whatever else we make of the twenty-first century. Clarke himself has noted, with a laugh, that if he had patented his wild idea back in 1945, he would be the richest man on the planet.

1946 ▶ Commercial failure of television

Darryl F. Zanuck

The General Electric Company was ready to introduce television commercially when World War II broke out, and the company's efforts were refocused to produce military equipment. Out in Hollywood, the studios prospered during the war, churning out movies to lift the spirits and to promote patriotism. When pre-war stars like Jimmy Stewart returned from enlistment duties after the war, however, they discovered that audience tastes had changed; *It's a Wonderful Life* was a flop when it was first released, for example. But not only did Hollywood have to discover a new style of movie-making, it also had to deal with the delayed advent of television.

In 1946, Darryl F. Zanuck, head of 20th Century Fox, pooh-poohed the new competitor, saying television wouldn't "be able to hold on to any market it captures after the first six months." Whether Zanuck actually believed this bit of wishful thinking is open to question. He also said, "People will soon get tired of staring at a plywood box," with a derisory tone, suggesting that he was simply trying to slow down sales of television sets. Whatever the motive, it was a spectacular miscall. It quickly became apparent that Americans were more than willing to stare at that plywood box for hours on end, and with so much entertainment available right there in the living room, box-office receipts for Hollywood movies plummeted. Zanuck, despite his bad call on the commercial viability of television, was one of the smartest men in Hollywood, and was quickest off the mark in devising a way to lure audiences back to the theaters. In 1952, he introduced the first major technical development since color pictures became common in the late 1930s: the wide-screen process called Cinemascope, which he launched with the splashy biblical epic *The Robe*. Even so, by the end of the decade the Hollywood studio system as it had existed since the 1920s was on the way out, and in the end, although movies proved they were around to stay, the remnants of the major studios found themselves deeply involved in producing shows for television, with Zanuck's old company leading the way.

1948 ▶ A world market for about five computers

Thomas J. Watson

This is one of the most quoted "laughably wrong" predictions on record. But in many ways, that is a bum rap. Thomas J. Watson was not a founder of IBM, but he was responsible for building it into the world leader in accounting machines in the 1930s, and for eventually leading it into the computer age. When Watson made his infamous remark, computers were both huge and hugely expensive. While there are competing claims to producing the first modern computer, the one that is most widely credited with primacy is ENIAC (Electronic Numerical Integrator and Calculator), which was built with government funding by J. Presper Eckert and John Mauchly, an engineer and a physicist at the University of Pennsylvania in Philadelphia. ENIAC was first demonstrated in 1946. Larger than a railroad boxcar, it had 18,000 vacuum tubes that had to be constantly replaced. What's more, although it could do 5,000 calculations a second, it was necessary to reset many switches and actually rewire certain elements if a different kind of calculation was required. The solution to that problem was to put the program instructions into the computer itself, as first suggested by the mathematician John von Neumann.

Mauchly and Eckert carried out this improvement in constructing UNIVAC. But it, too, was huge, and, just as Watson predicted, even the largest businesses were dubious about its usefulness. The U.S. Census Bureau began using one in 1951, and the public started to pay more attention when it came within six electoral votes of predicting Eisenhower's total of 432 in defeating Stevenson in 1952, a prediction made less than an hour after the polls closed. As soon as it became apparent that transistors— invented at Bell Laboratories by the future Nobel Prize– winning scientist William Shockley and his colleagues in 1947—could be used instead of vacuum tubes, thus greatly reducing the size of computers and solving many other problems as well, Watson got IBM aggressively involved in the commercial-computer business. The company began working on computers in the mid-1950s, and by 1964, now under the direction of Watson's son, IBM's $5 billion investment in what is known as scalable architecture— models of any size run by the same operating system— began to pay off, giving them eventual domination of the mainframe computer market. The company would later underestimate the appeal of personal computers, but that's another story (see 1977 and Ken Olsen). In terms of the senior Watson's initial prediction, he was, in fact, correct. UNIVACs were far from the wave of the future. Computers were, but in an entirely different form, and, when that form became clear, Watson immediately got into the fray.

Nevertheless, Watson can't be let off the hook altogether. That's because in 1937 the original notebooks of the long-forgotten "father" of the modern computer, Charles Babbage, were discovered and published. Babbage, born in London in 1791, had his first ideas about calculating mathematical tables mechanically in 1812. He subsequently built a small machine that calculated numbers to eight decimal places. In 1823, he managed to persuade the British government to provide funding for the construction of a machine that would calculate to twenty decimal places. In the mid-1830s, Babbage conceived an even more advanced calculator, which he called an "analytical engine." Using punched cards to retain mathematical information, the machine had a memory unit, sequential control, and several other features of modern computers. A professor at Cambridge University, Babbage again applied for government funding. The Chancellor of the Exchequer decided to consult the Astronomer Royal, Sir George Biddle Airy, on the matter, asking if such a machine could be of real value. Airy replied with one word: "Worthless."

Babbage's analytical engine was thus never built. But he busied himself with other projects, producing the first reliable actuarial tables, which proved of great value to insurance companies, and he helped to establish the British postal system. On a more mundane level, he invented the cowcatcher, the iron skirt attached to the front of steam locomotives to encourage cattle to get off the tracks. His analytical engine, however, which might have considerably speeded up the advent of the modern computer, was forgotten. But when his original notebooks were unearthed in 1937, they caused immense interest. Certainly Thomas Watson should have known about them, and been less dismissive of the future possibilities of computers.

Babbage's notebooks also revealed that his assistant in charge of the punched cards he had been experimenting with was none other than Lord Byron's daughter—which made her the first computer programmer. Babbage himself received vastly delayed vindication in 1991, when British scientists completed work on the construction, according to Babbage's exact specifications, of his Difference Engine #2. It proved accurate to thirty-one digits.

1948 "Dewey Defeats Truman"

Chicago Tribune

President Harry Truman was supposed to be a political dead duck in 1948. Even though he was credited with successfully guiding the nation through the final months of World War II, following the death of Franklin Delano Roosevelt, the postwar world was proving more unsettled than people had expected. The Soviet Union, under Stalin, had turned from an ally into a dangerous enemy, there was a new conflict in Korea to worry about, inflation was mounting at home, and the Democrats, after all, had now occupied the White House for sixteen years. In 1944, Roosevelt had defeated New York Governor Thomas Dewey because the voters had bought F.D.R.'s argument that it was unwise "to change horses in midstream" during a global conflict. But this time Dewey seemed like a sure thing. The pundits thought so, the newfangled national polls backed them up, and even many Truman stalwarts were pulling long faces. At times it seemed that only "Give 'Em Hell Harry" himself believed he could win. The *Chicago Tribune* took a look at the first results on election night and decided it was safe to go with a banner headline reading, DEWEY DEFEATS TRUMAN.

They were dead wrong. Truman held his own in the big states, splitting them with Dewey, and won in the farm states that were supposed to go Republican, as they usually did, except in Roosevelt's first two elections. But it turned out that the people of the Midwest trusted the man from Missouri, and were deeply suspicious of the slick Republican from the East. The joke that Dewey, who loved to wear tuxedos, looked like a "man on a wedding cake" proved to be particularly telling in rural areas, and the farmers went with Harry. That produced one of the most famous photographs in American political history, with a grinning Truman holding up a copy of the infamous early edition of the *Chicago Tribune*.

In the aftermath, the pollsters excused themselves by saying that they had really stopped polling five days before the election, and had missed a late shift to Truman. People bought that argument, and polling has played an ever-increasing role in elections ever since. Every election year, the polls get some congressional and gubernatorial results wrong, but since 1948 they have always had the correct winner in presidential contests, even when they got a state wrong here and there. They saved themselves from embarrassment in 1960 by calling it a toss-up between Kennedy and Nixon, and mostly have had an easy time of it, with considerable margins of error to count on. But then in 1996, they were once again off by a mile. They didn't get the winner wrong, which was why their mistake was given only a minor amount of attention by the media. Nevertheless, on the day before the 1996 vote, almost every major poll showed Clinton beating Dole by 16 points. In fact, the spread was only 8 points, with Ross Perot taking 10 percent. Thus, although polling had continued right up to the day before the election, the polls were even further off, in terms of actual numbers, than they had been in 1948. This suggests that polling isn't quite the science it pretends to be, and it remains possible that in the year 2000, or 2004, we will have another "Dewey Defeats Truman" headline. But even if that happened, we won't get a grin as infectious as Harry Truman's on election day in 1948. With television camera following their every step, politicians' grins have worn out their welcome long before election day.

1954 ► A space telescope

Lyman Spitzer, Jr.

Although it is named for the great American astronomer Edwin Hubble, who in 1925 was the first to show that the universe consisted of innumerable galaxies, the Hubble telescope owes its existence to Lyman Spitzer, Jr., as much as it does to anyone else. A renowned astrophysicist and plasma physicist, Spitzer advocated the launching of an earth satellite as early as 1947, the same year he became, at the age of thirty-two, professor of astronomy at Princeton University, as well as head of its astronomy department and director of its observatory. In 1954, he specifically suggested that a space observation point 500 miles above the Earth was the "next logical step" in observing the stars without the distortions presented by Earth's atmosphere.

Spitzer had many interests and made many important scientific contributions, from early work on sonar during World War II, ongoing research into the production of fusion power, and crucial theoretical work in astronomy that helped clarify many issues, including the nature of quasars. But his work in championing astronomical observations of space was at the center of his life. An ultraviolet observation satellite, the Copernicus Orbiting Astronomical Observatory, launched by NASA in 1972, was an early result of his advocacy in this field, and he headed the group of scientists that carried out its investigations. But, as *The New York Times* noted in his April 1997 obituary, "his crowning legacy was the Hubble Space Telescope, which can peer into the deepest reaches of space. His advocacy won over his peers and buoyed the $2.1 billion project through repeated delays." The Hubble Space Telescope was ready for launch in 1986, but the *Challenger* space shuttle disaster delayed lift-off until 1990. Problems with the original grinding of the telescope's lens necessitated repairs performed during a 1994 shuttle space walk, but since then the Hubble has provided the most breathtaking astronomical photographs ever seen, and allowed astronomers to look far deeper into space and time than ever before, moving us far closer to a glimpse of the creation of the universe in the original big bang. Robert W. Smith, a historian at the National Air and Space Museum, said at the time of the Hubble launch that Spitzer's "involvement in arguing for, justifying and then helping to develop the space telescope stretches back longer than the commitment of anyone else." Spitzer was the rare happy visionary to see his dream of the future come true.

1955 ▶ A nuclear-power utopia

Harold E. Stassen

In 1953, President Eisenhower started a program called "Atoms for Peace," designed to push the development of the peaceful uses of nuclear power, and to encourage public acceptance of atomic energy as something other than a weapon of mass destruction. The most enthusiastic promoter of these ideas was his special assistant on disarmament, Harold E. Stassen. Just before World War II, Stassen had been crowned as the "boy wonder" of American politics, having been elected governor of Wisconsin in his early thirties. Widely touted as a future president, he eventually became a laughing-stock by running for that office every four years for decades. But in the mid-1950s he was still taken seriously enough to be called on by the *Ladies' Home Journal* to expound on the administration's views concerning the future of nuclear power.

Stassen foresaw a future for nuclear energy that promised a world "in which there is no disease . . . where hunger is unknown . . . where 'dirt' is an old-fashioned word, and routine household tasks are just a matter of pushing a few buttons . . . a world where no one stokes a furnace or curses the smog, where the air is everywhere as fresh as on a mountaintop and the breeze from a factory is as sweet as a rose." Stassen always had a propensity for exaggeration, which was one reason why he eventually became an object of derision. But in the context of the 1950s, this hyperbole about the utopia that nuclear energy would bring didn't seem all that remarkable. For one thing, Stassen was drawing on ideas that went back a long way. As early as 1913, only a decade after scientists began to fully grasp the power inherent in the atom, H. G. Wells had written a novel called *The World Set Free*, in which a very similar utopia was imagined, although in this novel it came into being after an atomic war had nearly destroyed civilization.

In addition, Stassen's rosy vision was being echoed by many others. The founding publisher of *Life* and *Time*, Henry Luce, predicted in 1956 that by 1980 "all 'power' (electric, atomic, solar) is likely to be virtually costless." Even Walt Disney got into the act with "Tomorrowland Adventure," an animated short distributed free to public schools. This movie proclaimed that, "Atomic power has come just in time, for coal and oil are too valuable to burn." But by the end of the decade, the public was beginning to notice how long it took to construct a nuclear power plant and how much they cost to build. Beneath the surface, concerns about safety simmered. Atomic energy continued to have many champions, but it also had an increasing number of vocal critics. Utopian visions of the kind exemplified by Harold Stassen's fantasies of a perfect world faded from view, even in fiction. By the late 1970s, the idea of solar energy was more likely to engender excessive rhapsodies, and after the 1979 accident at the Three Mile Island nuclear plant, the proponents of nuclear power found themselves completely on the defensive.

1956 ▸ A mile-high skyscraper

Frank Lloyd Wright

In 1956, Frank Lloyd Wright produced a design for a mile-high skyscraper, to be built in Chicago and called the Illinois. It was to be 528 stories high, equipped with 56 atomic-powered elevators that could achieve top speeds of 60 miles per hour. Providing 17 million square feet of space, it was envisioned as housing 130,000 people. Some critics suspected that Wright was having everybody on, and satirizing the penchant for ever taller buildings. There had long been a school of thought that the height of skyscrapers was getting out of hand. In the early 1930s, a story in one of the science-fiction pulp magazines had envisioned a future in which such buildings were banned because of the collapse of a skyscraper— the owners of the penthouse apartment had gone on a trip around the world and left the bathwater running, causing the sealed structure to become so heavy that it toppled over, killing hundreds. But Wright insisted that he was serious, and that his building was completely sound structurally. He flatly predicted that it would stand longer than the pyramids of Egypt.

Wright's idea didn't die out, either. In the 1980s, the architect Robert Sobel and engineer Nat Krahl proposed a tower to be built in Houston, Texas, that was to be 500 stories and 1.3 miles high. This proposal unfortunately coincided with the depression in the Texas oil markets, and the building never got off the ground, as it were. Buckminster Fuller *really* wanted to get off the ground. In the 1960s, he proposed a floating city. Using the principles of his geodesic domes, the Sky City would be a half mile across and enclosed in an aluminum shell. The heat of the sun, he said, would cause the air inside the enormous aluminum ball to expand enough so that some of it would be expelled, lifting the structure into the atmosphere. This, he suggested, might be a good way for Japan, with its restricted land area, to provide additional living space. He did admit that the construction of such a city lay several decades in the future. It has since been suggested that such a Sky City might more appropriately be built on the moon, where the lower gravity would make it easier to launch. But it seems more likely that we will have a mile-high skyscraper in the Wright mold on the surface of the Earth before we get around to colonizing the moon.

1956 ▸ Absurdity of space travel

Richard van der Riet-Wooley

Upon his investiture as British Astronomer Royal, perhaps the most coveted scientific post in the British Empire, one that almost always led to an eventual knighthood, Dr. Richard van der Riet-Wooley delivered himself of pronouncements on a number of topics. The British were all too well acquainted with rocketry, having been bombarded by German V-2 missiles during World War II. But post-war speculation about the use of rockets for space travel was too much for Riet-Wooley. "Space travel," said the new Astronomer Royal, "is utter bilge."

A few months later, in October 1956, the Soviet Union launched the first artificial satellite, "Sputnik." But that was an object only 23 inches in diameter, and even though it caused a world-wide sensation, and deeply embarrassed the United States, which was supposedly far ahead in rocket development, it was still a far cry from space travel. The Soviet rocket programs were a state secret, and the experiments of the United States, conducted more publicly, often met with failure. The only segment of the general public that seemed to believe in the inevitability of space travel were readers of science fiction. This genre of fiction was dismissed by most literary critics as "pulp" and "space opera"; novels like Aldous Huxley's *Brave New World* and George Orwell's *1984* were taken seriously because they could be tucked into the category of utopian speculation, which had a long history in Western literature. But it was in fact the readers of science fiction, especially of the stories and novels published in John E. Campbell's scientifically oriented *Astounding Science Fic-*

tion, who had the surest grasp of the future. In his history of science fiction, *The Trillion Year Spree,* Brian Aldiss writes: "One thing *Astounding* had which can never be recaptured. It had faith. The peculiar faith that space travel was possible and would come about. This belief has long ago been translated into fact. At the time, however, in the forties and fifties, it was greeted with almost universal skepticism or ignorance. To be a part of Campbell's audience was to feel oneself a member of a privileged minority who knew in their bones what was going to happen in the future."

When Sputnik was launched, science-fiction readers were ecstatic—the future was beginning. They didn't know about the grim meeting at the White House the day after Sputnik appeared in the sky, a meeting at which President Eisenhower conferred with military and scientific leaders to discuss how the United States could catch up with the Soviet Union in space science. But they knew some such meeting must be taking place—now things would really begin to happen. When they did, the Soviets were again first. On April 12, 1961, Soviet Army Major Yuri Gagarin was launched into space. The future was already here. The science-fiction fans had been correct. To tweak the Astronomer Royal, the British Interplanetary Society put out a special bulletin announcing that Yuri Gagarin had been launched "into utter bilge." An embarrassed van der Riet-Wooley replied that he had not been talking about real science, but about the nonsense published in science-fiction magazines. This remark only made matters worse, and guaranteed that his 1956 statement would become one of the most quoted predictive mistakes in the annals of the conquest of space.

1957 ▶ Proof of Martian life in rock found in the Arctic

James Blish

A major science-fiction writer of the 1950s to the 1970s, James Blish published a novel in 1957 titled *The Frozen Year*. In it the hero, Farnsworth, makes an expedition to the North Pole. He finds a pebble in a piece of ice that he keeps frozen until his return to civilization. Analysis of the pebble reveals that it is a tektite from the asteroid belt. It consists of a stone that is sedimentary in nature, indicating the presence of water. As the novel unfolds, he learns that it is a tiny remnant of a former planet destroyed in a war of the worlds by a Martian civilization, leading Farnsworth to exclaim, "Cosmic history in an ice cube!"

In August 1996, NASA made a bombshell announcement concerning a rock that had been found in the Antarctic. One of a group of meteorite fragments found in 1984 and called SNCs (pronounced "snicks" and short for Shergotty-Nakhla-Chassigny) had been analyzed to reveal a potentially epochal secret. At the August news conference, the head of NASA, Dan Goldin, began by saying, "Today we are on the threshold of establishing whether life is unique to earth." Then NASA scientists began discussing the rock lying on a blue velvet cushion on the dais. Several things about the rock had been established beyond question by various kinds of testing. It had been formed on Mars about 4.5 billion years ago. After the passage of a half billion years, the rock, which had lain below the surface, was exposed to water when meteorites had cracked the Martian surface. A mere

16 million years ago, an object from space, perhaps an asteroid, had been large enough to send part of the Martian crust flying into space when it impacted, and then this particular piece of that crust had finally fallen to Earth in Antarctica only 16,000 years ago, where it had remained embedded in the ice until 1984.

Analysis of the rock had shown the presence of carbonates similar to those that are formed by bacteria on Earth. There were also fine-grained iron sulfides and other minerals that had a resemblance to bacterial products. A third kind of material found in concentration represented a common chemical resulting from the decay of bacteria. What's more, an electron-scanning microscope revealed tiny structures of two different shapes that NASA scientists believed could be fossils of Martian bacteria. Having said that much, worthy of huge headlines around the globe, NASA was careful to have a scientist on hand at the news conference to explain why he didn't believe these were fossilized remnants of Martian bacteria because they were too small even by microscopic standards, and because the carbonates appeared to have been created at temperatures far too high to permit life.

Many of the newspaper headlines, of course, ignored all this caution and simply screamed LIFE ON MARS! In the months since, scientists have weighed in with many opinions supporting and questioning the possibility that remnants of ancient Martian bacteria are involved. The arguments are highly technical and not likely to settle the matter, anyway. To do that, many scientists say, it would be necessary to slice one of these infinitesimal fossils open to show the existence of a cell wall, or better yet, cell division. But the techniques for doing such microscopic surgery are still under development. In the meantime, there has been a new upsurge of debate about whether such bacteria, if they once existed, could still exist beneath the arid surface of Mars. The Mars rock "bacteria" have also given new impetus to planned robotic surveys of the planet, and enhanced the ever-present dream of human expeditions to the Red Planet. For as James Blish's hero proclaimed back in 1957, what we have here is a suggestion of "Cosmic history in an ice cube."

1961 ▶ Castro soon overthrown

The Kiplinger Washington Letter

For decades, *The Kiplinger Washington Letter* had a good reputation as an economic- and political-insider tip-sheet, where you could read about the news before it happened. This weekly newsletter got a great many forecasts right over the years, but by its editors' own admission, when it made a mistake it was often a beaut. One of those was a forecast published on February 18, 1961: "Castro in Cuba will be overthrown within months." The newsletter reported that a revolutionary force of Cuban exiles was training in Guatemala for an invasion of Cuba, and that the United States had agreed not to "interfere with the movement of the troops by water."

On April 17, 1961, 1500 anti-Castro troops did indeed land at Cuba's Bay of Cochinos. They had been trained by the United States Central Intelligence Agency, but the invasion fell apart within a few days. Not only did a lack of supplies hamper the invaders, but instead of being aided by uprisings within Cuba itself, massive Cuban forces fought against them. This debacle went down in history as the Bay of Pigs incident. Although it had initially been planned during the Eisenhower administration, John F. Kennedy, in office only three months, publicly accepted full responsibility for the disaster on April 24, gaining a reputation for being forth-right in the process.

Periodic predictions that Castro was about to be over-thrown have surfaced again and again in the thirty-five years since the Bay of Pigs; even *The Kiplinger Washington Letter* has made the same mistake all over again. But as of the spring of 1997, Castro was still in charge, surviving even the breakup of his sponsor, the Soviet Union, and becoming the longevity champ among all communist dictators.

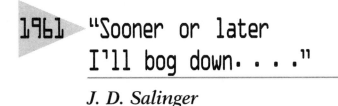

1961 "Sooner or later I'll bog down. . . ."

J. D. Salinger

In 1961 two stories by J. D. Salinger that had originally been published by *The New Yorker* were published in book form. On the dust jacket of *Franny and Zooey* Salinger wrote of himself, "There is a real enough danger, I suppose, that sooner or later I'll bog down, per-haps disappear entirely, in my own methods, locutions and mannerisms. On the whole, though, I'm very hope-ful." Reading those words today, it is difficult not to won-der if he was lying to us when he said he was hopeful. Because since then there has been only one more story, followed by decades of seclusion and silence.

Writers do run out of steam sometimes, as E. M. Forster did. Others stop publishing because of a sense of rejec-tion, as happened with Herman Melville. After the popu-lar success of early novels like *Typee* and *Redburn*, *Moby-Dick* was a comparative failure and *Pierre* a disaster.

Melville did write *Billy Budd* after that, but he put it away in a trunk where it was finally discovered a half century later, in the early 1920s, and immediately recognized as a masterpiece. But J. D. Salinger met with no such rejection. True, the *New York Times Book Review* originally panned *The Catcher in the Rye*: "This book, though, it's too long. Gets kind of monotonous. And he should have cut out a lot about these jerks and all at that crumby school. They depress me." But most reviewers saw right away that it was an American classic, and it was immensely popular. Indeed, Salinger's legion of fans have always been mad at him for holding out on them, for refusing to publish whatever he was writing all these many years.

But has he been writing? Rumors say yes, but it's hard to know. Most people thought Truman Capote really was writing his novel *Answered Prayers* in the last years of his life, but it turned out he hadn't been. A great many readers fervently hope that Salinger has been writing, but just not publishing the result. They want to believe that the "disappearance" he predicted for himself was just a matter of being reclusive and not of being so bogged down in his own methods that no words have been getting put on paper. He's an old man now. Before too long we'll know how complete the disappearance he predicted has really been.

1961 ▸ Terraforming other planets

Carl Sagan

Carl Sagan was not only a respected scientist but one of the most important popularizers of scientific knowledge in the second half of the twentieth century. The author of numerous best-selling books, he was probably best known for his PBS series *Cosmos*. Wearing his scientific hat, Sagan was the first person to seriously discuss the idea of terraforming other planets—making them habitable for human beings by transforming their existing conditions. In a scientific article he wrote in 1961, Sagan noted that current research showed Venus to have a surface temperature "well above the normal boiling point of water, produced by a carbon dioxide/water vapor greenhouse effect." As he recounts in his 1994 book *Pale Blue Dot*, Sagan proposed seeding the planet's clouds with genetically engineered microorganisms that, over time and through a variety of chemical processes, would make the surface of the planet habitable.

Science fiction writers had long been imagining human communities on alien planets, of course, but these settlements or cities were conveniently located on planets that already had a fundamentally earth like aspect, or else the process by which they had been made habitable was largely ignored. That changed after the publication of Sagan's article. "The idea was soon taken up," he writes, "by a number of science fiction authors in the continuing dance between science and science fiction—in which the science stimulated the fiction, and the fiction stimulates a new generation of scientists, a process benefiting both genres." Sagan ruefully notes that as more was learned about Venus, including the fact that its clouds are made of sulfuric acid, it became clear that his original scheme would not work.

But the *idea* of terraforming other planets survived, not only in science fiction stories, but in the world of real science. Plans for expeditions to Mars developed by NASA and by international consortiums, consider the eventual terraforming of the planet in great technical detail, beginning with ways to use the planet's own resources to support initial domed communities. Further in the future, it is believed by many scientists that several moons of the outer planets, particularly Neptune's Triton, are viable candidates for eventual terraforming. Such enormous and hugely expensive projects may not get under way for decades, perhaps not even in the twenty-first century. But terraforming is now a part of the fundamental vocabulary of future space exploration.

1962 The end of the world

Hindu astrologers

In his book *The 20th Century*, David Wallechinsky provides a rundown of numerous end-of-the-world predictions, under the heading "Armageddon Outa Here." Most of these involve rather small cults, but the 1962 prediction by Hindu astrologers caused widespread panic in India. According to the astrologers, "For the first time in four centuries, eight planets were due to line up in a spectacular planetary conjunction as they entered the House of Capricorn." Although the idea that the world would end was laughed off by Prime Minister

Nehru, "throughout the whole subcontinent millions gathered in nonstop prayer meetings in hopes of calming the anger of the gods." When the world did not end, the prayers were, of course, given credit, as they always are in these cases.

Visions of Armageddon crop up in every culture, and have done so throughout human history. In the Christian West, the Bible's book of Revelation is a perennial source of such predictions. Many Christians do not realize, however, how strong a role such ideas played in Christian history. Once the Christian religion had been accepted by the Roman Emperor Constantine, and began to spread through Europe, three distinct strains of belief were in competition for primacy, with different theologies derived from St. Jerome, St. Paul, and St. Augustine. The theology connected with St. Jerome was an apocalyptic one. It held that the end of the world and the Second Coming were almost upon the world, and that all men and women should remain virgins in order to enter into heaven. This theology had problems. First, since the world kept right on going through succeeding generations, doubts about the validity of the Christian religion as a whole were fostered. Secondly, lifelong virginity seemed too high a price to pay for entry into heaven, at least from the viewpoint of most people. During the Middle Ages, therefore, prelates struggled to decide upon a consistent theology for the whole of the Catholic church. Although St. Jerome had his advocates, the choice eventually came down to a decision between the followers of St. Paul and those of St. Augustine. If the views of St. Jerome were too rigid, those of St. Augustine were seen as perhaps too lax. His famous call to the Lord to be saved, "but not yet," so that he could sow some wild oats, was seen as lacking in discipline. Thus St. Paul, who had said that it was "better to marry than to burn" (burn with lust, not burn in hell) was chosen as representing "the middle way." The codification at Ghent laid the groundwork of modern Catholicism.

But the strain of apocalyptic thinking exemplified by St. Jerome did not go away, and these days survives in several Protestant religions. The Reverend Pat Robertson, the Christian Right leader who ran for president in 1988, is on record as having predicted the end of the world several times. When it does not occur, he credits the intervention of prayer and moves the date up. At last report, we can relax until the year 2003.

1964 ▶ The Beatles won't be an American hit

Alan Livingston

As John, Paul, George, and Ringo were about to make their first trip to America, the president of Capitol Records, their U.S. label, said, "We don't think they'll do anything in this market." Alan Livingston liked their music, but thought the Beatles' haircuts—those bangs—and their neat little black suits, were all wrong for the United States. But from the moment they arrived at Kennedy Airport on February 7, 1964, there was a kind of hysteria in the air. The teenage girls who had flooded the audience for the February 9 appearance on *The Ed Sullivan Show* screamed so loudly and incessantly that the music could hardly be heard. Their first American concert, at Carnegie Hall in New York on February 12, almost caused a riot on 57th Street, and the great popular phenomenon of the second half of the twentieth century was under way.

The only album immediately available was *Meet the Beatles*, but Capitol rushed their previous recordings into release, and by the first week of April, the group held the first five slots on America's Top 10 list. "Can't Buy Me Love" was number 1, followed by "Twist and Shout," "She Loves You," "I Want to Hold Your Hand," (in release since January) and "Please Please Me." The following week they had fourteen songs listed on the Hot 100, a feat that has never since even been approached. They returned to the United States in August for a thirty-six-city tour, beginning in San Francisco, that was a howling success.

It is doubtful that anyone had ever been so happy to have made a wrong prediction as Capitol's Alan Livingston.

1965 The Library of Congress in a few filing cabinets

Popular Science

In 1965 *Popular Science* published an article on the possibilities inherent in the new developments in the field of microfilm, which it called "Putting a Library in a Shoebox." "How would you like to have the Library of Congress, occupying 270 miles of bookshelves, in your home?" the article asked. "Sounds impossible? Well, through a new microphotography process, you may, one day, be able to have the entire contents of the great library in your den on film—all contained in about six filing cabinets."

Notice the discrepancy between the six filing cabinets mentioned in the text and the shoebox of the title. Even science magazines cannot resist the kind of hype more usually associated with "revolutionary" diet plans. The article's question, "Sounds impossible?" is a lot nearer the mark. It's not that the entire Library of Congress couldn't be put on microfilm, technologically speaking, but simply that it would require something akin to the kind of *carte blanche* funding available to NASA during the Apollo program to land an American on the moon. Such money was not, of course, made available. Indeed, funding for American libraries across the board, including the Library of Congress, has been declining since the early 1980s, shunted to the back alleys of Ronald Reagan's "shining city on a hill." In the more than thirty years since the *Popular Science* article, less than 10 percent of the Library's holdings have made it onto microfilm. And in most public libraries around the nation, you will be lucky to find the last fifteen years of *The New York Times* and the local newspaper available in that format.

Despite that failure, a newer and better "shoebox" is now being hyped: the Internet. As of the beginning of 1997, the Library of Congress had managed to raise nearly $24 million from foundations and other private sources, and pried a commitment for an additional $15 million out of Congress to make its holdings available on the Internet. But which holdings? Not its more than 20 million books. Despite the visionary claims of some Internet prophets, almost nobody seems to be reading books on their screens, and downloading the several hundred pages of a Dickens novel in unbound pages doesn't seem to be the wave of the future either. Quite sensibly, what the Library is making available is material from its nonbook collections, including everything from the papers of the first twenty-three presidents to newspaper cartoons and theatre posters.

This is a splendid idea, and it has had great initial success. The Library Web site is already attracting about 5 million "hits" a week, many of them from schoolchildren. As of March 1997, they can choose from about 300,000 different items, and the goal is to put 5 million items online by the year 2000. That's an enormous amount of material to be able to access. But in terms of the *Popular Science* shoebox prediction, it should be noted that the nonbook holdings of the Library of Congress total 70 million items. The fairly modest goal the Library has set itself is both worthy and reasonable. Still, those who claim that the Internet promises to become an all-encompassing repository of human knowledge should take note that the current goals of the Library are in fact modest, and should remember the microfilm shoebox.

1966 ▸ An end to the Vietnam War

President Lyndon Baines Johnson

On September 21, 1966, Lyndon Johnson looked into the television cameras and said, "I believe there is a light at the end of what has been a long and lonely tunnel." The phrase about the light at the end of the tunnel had been swiped from the columnist Joseph Alsop, who had used the metaphor the previous week. It was a phrase that got picked up and repeated like a mantra again and again over the next several years; eventually it would be used sardonically, as a way of saying, "Yeah, right."

The Vietnam War was the most heartbreaking in American history. Both Lyndon Johnson and his successor, Richard Nixon, told intimates that they were damned if they'd be the first U.S. President to lose a war, and so refused to pay attention to the ever more clamorous protests in the streets and on college campuses, or to listen to those Washington insiders who suggested that America should just declare victory and come home. At the beginning of the American Civil War, both sides expected it to be over quickly, but it dragged on for four long years. At the beginning of World War I, both sides expected the conflict to end in a matter of weeks, and again it went on for four years. People seemed to have learned their lesson by World War II, and knew they were in it for the long haul. But even then, no one really thought Germany could hold out for almost another year if the D-Day invasion of June 1944 succeeded. But nothing dragged on like the Vietnam War. From the dispatch of the first few hundred American "advisers" to Vietnam in 1957, to the fall of Saigon in January 1973, when the last American officials were evacuated by helicopter, almost sixteen years had passed. And we were told again and again that there "was light at the end of the tunnel."

1968 ▶ A coming "plutonium economy"

Glenn Seaborg

Glenn Seaborg was one of the discoverers of plutonium, the previously unknown metallic element that was produced when an atom of uranium-238 absorbed a neutron. He was in charge of the production of plutonium during the race to develop the first atomic bomb under the Manhattan Project. Plutonium was given its name because it fell two places beyond uranium on the periodic table of elements, just as the planet Pluto was two steps beyond Uranus, for which uranium was also named. As many historians of the dawn of the nuclear age have pointed out, the scientists involved in the Manhattan Project were concerned about the destructive power of the forces they were unleashing, and were far from unaware of the ironic symbolism of naming the new metal after the Roman god of the underworld.

Seaborg later served for ten years as the chairman of the Atomic Energy Commission. In that position, he recommended to President Kennedy in 1962 that the United States concentrate on the development of what were called breeder reactors, because they produced new supplies of plutonium, for nuclear power plants. Breeder reactors were more expensive and presented more technical and safety problems than plants that made use of uranium-235 that had been separated out from natural uranium ore, but Seaborg felt strongly that plutonium would be essential to future power production. In later speeches, including one at the twenty-fifth anniversary of Washington's Hanford-Richland nuclear facility, which had been established during the Manhattan Project along with Oak Ridge and Los Alamos, Seaborg talked in 1968 of plutonium becoming so fundamentally important to the world economy that the metal might replace gold as the international monetary standard.

This prophecy reverberated strongly within the scientific community. Back in 1901, when Frederick Soddy and Ernest Rutherford had first discovered that radioactivity was an indication that a basic change in matter was taking place, Soddy had cried out in excitement, "Rutherford, this is transmutation." Rutherford had immediately warned him not to use the word "transmutation," because of its historic association with that scientific black sheep known as alchemy, one of the principal aims of which was to transmute lead into gold. Gradually, the term "transmutation" came to be accepted in connection with nuclear physics, and Rutherford even used the word in a book title thirty years later. But for Seaborg to now suggest that a plutonium standard might eventually replace the gold standard was to give the ancient concept of transmutation a new spin.

In fact, of course, Seaborg's vision of a plutonium economy would be derailed by increasing public anxiety about the safety of nuclear power plants, which would be greatly elevated in only eleven years from Seaborg's speech by the accident at Three Mile Island. Furthermore, the disposal of nuclear wastes from power plants, including spent plutonium, became a major public issue that has had Congress tied in knots to this day.

1968 ▶ Picturephones

Arthur C. Clarke and Stanley Kubrick

Prototypes of picturephones, which would allow callers to see each other on a screen at the same time they conversed telephonically, were demonstrated at the 1963–1964 World's Fair. But it was not until five years later, with the release of the movie *2001: A Space Odyssey*, that the idea came across to the public with full impact. Millions of moviegoers around the world were struck by the scene in which an American scientist, stopping off at the great ringed space station on his way to the moon, places a call home to Earth and has a conversation with his young daughter, whom he can see squirming around in the living room as they talk. In a movie overflowing with technological marvels, this was the one thing moviegoers could easily imagine doing themselves a few years down the line. In writing the script, Arthur C. Clarke, upon whose short story "The Sentinel" the movie was based, and Stanley Kubrick, who also directed, had deliberately included this scene as something the viewer could quickly grasp before being taken on the futuristic ride of their lives. AT&T and Bell Laboratories cooperated in providing the hardware for this scene exactly because they wanted to whet people's appetites for what they saw as a major new commercial product in the near future.

But it took another twenty years to make the picturephone practical; digital signal processing had to be developed first. Once they did become practical, AT&T found to its dismay that the public didn't really want them after all. As *The New York Times* reported in January 1997, "Picturephones are the very model of technology-driven future vision that came to nothing." Part of the problem was that by the time they were available for test-marketing, there was a public backlash against even the supposed felicities of answering machines; most people agreed that answering machines were essential to modern life, but at the same time almost everybody hated them, especially when making a call and getting the machine instead of the person being called. But test-marketing revealed an even bigger problem as well. People at home don't want to be seen when they answer the phone. They want to be able to answer the phone and not have the caller know that their hair is a mess or that they're wearing torn T-shirts or even nothing at all. Assurances that the picture could be kept turned off didn't work. Too many people could hear their mothers or mothers-in-law saying, "Why are you hiding from me?" Too many people could imagine bosses or neighbors or salespeople staring at them with prying eyes. The "Big Brother" of George Orwell's novel *1984* had a way of popping into people's heads. In a world in which privacy was increasingly at a premium, picturephones were simply not what consumers wanted.

Video teleconferencing is used increasingly by businesses, but that is a very controlled context in which everyone is at pains to look their best anyway. It is also possible, if not yet easy, to link personal computers and digital cameras to send live video over the Internet. That is likely to become a standard option in the near future, although there are those who think it may be more associated with sex chat rooms than anything else—in which case Congress is likely to step in. At any rate, the picturephone as seen in *2001* appears to be a prediction that didn't pan out because it came to be seen as more of a threat than a promise.

1968 ▸ Artificial intelligence

Arthur C. Clarke and Stanley Kubrick

The term "artificial intelligence" (AI) came out of a 1956 conference at Dartmouth College, but for the general public and computer scientists alike, the first full-scale vision of future possibilities came with the supercomputer called HAL in the movie *2001: A Space Odyssey*. What Arthur C. Clarke and Stanley Kubrick imagined in their script, so brilliantly brought to life in Kubrick's direction, was a computer so completely endowed with humanlike intelligence that it became a character in itself. Indeed, HAL often seemed more human than the extremely unemotional crew members played by Keir Dullea and Gary Lockwood. It was HAL, of course, that went "mad," and the scene in which his higher functions were turned off, concluding with his statement that he had been born on January 12, 1992 (1997 in the original script) and singing the song "Daisy," the first thing he had been taught, was for many the most moving moment in the film.

No science-fiction film has even been more rigorously scientific than *2001*, but it was also extremely optimistic about the speed with which technology would develop. The huge space station and lavish moon base it depicts are not beyond reason, if we had the will and the willingness to invest the vast funds required, but HAL in particular remains pure fiction. Indeed, there are many computer scientists who doubt that the human race will ever be able to build the likes of HAL. The difficulty is not just a technological one. In fact, as T*he New York Times* has noted, "HAL's hardware capability has long since been realized: Supercomputer speeds, parallel processing and multitasking are realities today." The fact that the human brain has at least ten trillion circuits is in itself daunting, but the real problem is that we haven't even begun to understand how those circuits interact.

In *High-Tech Society*, Tom Forrester described artificial-intelligence research as covering "the broad areas of expert systems, robotics, speech recognition, image processing, and the attempt to discover the rules by which humans think (sometimes called 'applied epistemology')." An expert system "tells the computer what to do without specifying how to do it . . . The 'how' and 'why' of the system are kept separate." The intellectual system used by expert systems is formally called "heuristics," but its informal description tells more about the difficulties: it's a matter of making good guesses. Good guesses. That's how the human intelligence works, but it is fearsomely difficult to get a machine to do the same when we don't even know how most of our own guesses are arrived at, or why they actually work a lot of the time. There are narrowly defined expert systems in use, doing such things as analyzing chemical compounds and facilitating aircraft design. Even Campbell's Soup has an expert system for quality control. But these are very narrow applications, small corners of what we regard as intelligence.

The most complex expert system yet devised is Deep Blue, the computer that played chess master Gary Kasparov. Designed by C. J. Tan and his colleagues at IBM, it was beaten in February 1996 by Kasparov despite the fact that it could compute 200 million moves per second to Kasparov's 2. It won the first game, but when Kasparov changed his strategy, and altered his "style" of playing, Deep Blue was confounded. It didn't understand style. HAL, of course, was able to beat Keir Dullea at chess in *2001*, and this is an area in which computers ought to be able to excel. Deep Blue was altered to deal with the "style" problem and in a rematch in May 1997, Deep Blue beat Kasparov. Even so, that matches only one of HAL's thousands of abilities. As Roger C. Schank of Northwestern University has written, "The ability to play chess is deceptively complex, whereas the ability to understand English is deceptively simple."

Speech recognition is in fact proving to be a major problem—so far computers can recognize only a few hundred words and have trouble with accents and inflections. There is a great deal of argument within the community of computer scientists about whether artificial intelligence on the level imagined for HAL is ever going to be possible. Even though Deep Blue can calculate 200 million chess moves a second, scientists believe that across the full range of intelligence, the human brain parallel-processes millions of billions of calculations a second. All that Deep Blue is doing is playing chess; a Gary Kasparov is doing millions of other things, just to stay alive, at the same time he is playing chess. And we don't really know how he—or any other human being— does almost any of it.

1970 ▶ Mass starvation

Paul R. Erlich

In his 1970 book, *The Population Bomb*, Paul R. Erlich wrote, "The battle to feed all humanity is over. . . . At this late date, nothing can prevent a substantial increase in the world death rate." Erlich had serious academic credentials, to bolster his argument that the birthrate around the world had already passed the point where anything could prevent mass starvation in Africa and Asia. Although his predictions were apocalyptic and his tone sometimes strident, his warning was taken very seriously in many quarters. Numerous experts backed him up, and even extended the scope of the warning. A few years later, a publication of the World Future Society quoted the Scandinavian scientist Gota Ehrenswaerd's prediction that between 2020 and 2050 a "population crash" would occur, due to starvation, that would kill seven billion people, bringing the world population back to the barely sustainable 1970 level of three billion. To hammer the point home, some statisticians pointed out that the rate of increase would mean that in a few hundred thousand years, every centimeter of the known universe, planets, moon, stars, and the vacuum in between would be taken up by human beings.

But that kind of talk tended to backfire, reducing the argument to absurdity. What's more, there were many forces arrayed against drastic measures to curtail population. The adamant opposition to birth control on the part of the Vatican, fundamentalist religious beliefs that Armageddon was inevitable anyway (with heaven having infinite room for the saved), and the difficulty of thinking in terms of billions of anything except stars and dollars, all played their part. In third world countries, having great numbers of children continued to be seen as an old-age insurance policy—maybe one or two children would survive to care for their elderly parents. Many Americans took the attitude that we had our population level under control, ignoring the point made by Erlich and others that every American child, on average, consumed three times as much energy, food, and raw materials as a child in a third world country. And conservative American politicians who were both antiabortion and anti-foreign aid, campaigned and voted to cut off funds for birth control programs that even mentioned the word *abortion*.

In the meantime, China made enormous efforts to bring its population, the world's largest, under control. The idea of a government telling people how many children it could have made Westerners uncomfortable, and the fact that it involved enforced abortion did not sit well even with prochoice advocates. Word that Chinese peasants were killing newborn girls, because a son was regarded as so much more desirable, was met with horror. And it is only recently that the West has become fully aware that China's program of population control also involved the deliberate starving of millions of people.

Thus while the need for population control remains obvious to large numbers of people, the means to this end remain a matter of contention. In advanced societies, there tends to be a feeling that the whole problem would go away if people would just be sensible. Periodic onslaughts of televised pictures of babies starving in Africa arouse feelings of guilt and an intermittent understanding that Erlich's warning of a quarter century ago has to a degree already come true—mass starvation is, in fact, occurring right now, and has been going on for decades. But many people prefer to hear the more optimistic voices noting that new technologies and genetically improved grains make it possible to feed more people with crops grown on less land every year. Reports that more third world women are availing themselves of modern birth control methods also act as a palliative. Yet the successors to Paul Erlich continue to warn that water, the world's most precious resource, is increasingly scarce, and that all it will take to bring on catastrophe is the kind of drought, in the wrong places, that created the American dustbowl in the 1930s. The predictions of mass starvation that began in the 1970s are still far from being deemed false.

1971 Environmental catastrophe

Barry Commoner

In his 1971 book, *The Closing Circle*, Barry Commoner wrote, "My own judgment, based on the evidence now at hand, is that the present course of environmental degradation, at least in industrial countries, represents a challenge to essential ecological systems that is so serious that, if continued, it will destroy the capability of the environment to support a reasonably civilized human society. Some number of human beings might well survive such a catastrophe, for the collapse of civilization would reduce the pace of environmental degradation."

This apocalyptic vision of future catastrophe was made more persuasive by the fact that Commoner was very adept at questioning his own premises before others could do so. He admitted the many difficulties of forecasting the results of factors ranging from population growth to chemical residues. Because he seemed to give opposing views a fair shake, *The Closing Circle* did not have the ranting quality that can so easily undermine calls for reform. At the same time, however, he kept coming back to his central theme that civilization itself was seriously threatened by the technology and greed of humankind. And although he blunted the attacks of critics by acknowledging some of their stands, he certainly did not succeed in shutting them up altogether. Many politicians, industrial leaders, and scientific experts of various stripes said that he was vastly overstating the dangers at hand. The case against Commoner's brand of warning was then, and remains today, based largely on two points: One, it can't be proved that things are that bad. And two, human ingenuity will overcome whatever truly serious problems do arise.

It is interesting to note that Commoner was writing before evidence was developed to show that the ozone layer that protects the earth from excessive ultraviolet rays was shrinking. He devotes only a few scattered paragraphs to this subject that, for more than a decade now, has been a central concern of scientists involved in environmental studies. While it has been shown that holes in the ozone layer do appear for several months of the year, the fact that they then disappear has meant that there is still a major argument on the significance of the damage being done. Much debate still swirls around many other environmental subjects as well.

It is also true that much progress has been made in reducing the pollutants that could lead to environmental degradation beyond a point of no return. Indeed, the environmental movement has never been stronger, particularly in the western United States. A good deal of that progress, and heightened environmental consciousness, can certainly be attributed to Barry Commoner and others like him. Just as Rachel Carson's famous book *Silent Spring* alerted a broad public to the horrendous side-effects of DDT, leading to its ultimately being banned in the United States, so *The Closing Circle* had had a tremendous influence on public and private thinking about the environment. Both Carson's and Commoner's books had the effect of opening people's eyes to serious problems that had not received sufficient attention. When a book by someone with genuine credentials becomes a best-seller, the warnings of future catastrophe it contain can sometimes be powerful enough to cause changes that alter the future. Such warnings cannot then be dismissed as incorrect because their bleak scenarios have not come true. Rather, it needs to be recognized that the disasters such writers envision have not occurred exactly because the warning was sufficiently cogent to bring about real changes. In the case of environmental degradation, great problems remain, and it is too soon to completely discount Commoner's prediction that civilization will collapse. But if it does not, it will be in part because he issued his warning in the first place.

1971 The "office of the future"

Xerox scientists

In 1971, a team of Xerox scientists and programmers hatched the idea of "the office of the future," a pristine environment with a much reduced staff and almost no paper files in which practically everything was done by computers. The concept received a great deal of play in the popular press, and entirely new subsidiaries, including Exxon Office Systems in the United States and

Nexos in England, were created to take commercial advantage of the concept, and to develop the necessary hardware and software. But this was one of those famous "ideas whose time has come" that prove to be unworkable in practice.

A basic problem that no one had initially taken into account was that most existing skyscrapers could not be properly wired to carry the electronic load. Entirely new structures were discovered to be necessary; because of the long lead time involved in the construction of skyscrapers, even new buildings scheduled to go up years later could not be sufficiently altered to handle the problem. While the advent of personal computers at first seemed likely to move the concept forward, incompatibility of components and the ruthless technological competition that developed turned out to undermine the basic premise. Long before the compatibility problems even began to be solved, either technically or legally, Nexos had gone bankrupt in England, and subsidiaries like Exxon Office Systems had been sold off to fend for themselves.

Moreover, new computer technology sometimes had the reverse effect on the amount of paper used in offices from what had been expected. As numerous experts have pointed out, the increased efficiency with which reports and proposals could be turned out on word processors simply led to more drafts being done than ever before. The age-old problem of executives asking for changes in the copy just to demonstrate their own importance became even worse. In the past, contracts had been standard legal documents with blank spaces in which the particular of any given deal could be typed in. With word processors in use, each contract could be specifically tailored to the case at hand—but that meant that lawyers had to read every word of a contract instead of merely checking the typed-in details in an otherwise all-purpose text. This not only took more time, but often led to the work being divided up, which meant more copies floating around the office.

But nothing played as much havoc with the vision of a "paperless" office of the future as e-mail. While laws have been passed to help control the onslaught of unsolicited e-mail in the form of junk advertising, the amount of paper generated by this often useful technology seems to many experts to be spiraling out of control. The highly respected chairman of Computer Associates, Charles Wang, has gone so far as to shut down his company's e-mail system for five hours a day so his employees can actually get some real work done.

Thus while there are more computers, doing more things at an ever faster rate in modern offices around the world, the pristine, "paperless" environment envisioned by the Xerox team in 1971 has been filed in that overflowing container called a wastebasket.

1974 Chlorofluorocarbons will destroy ozone layer

F. Sherwood Rowland

In 1970, Harold Johnston of the University of California at Berkeley issued a warning that the nitrogen oxides that would be released as exhaust from the planned Supersonic Transport could damage the stratospheric ozone layer that protects the earth from the sun's ultraviolet rays. Although the high cost of these planes had already dimmed prospects that the United States government would underwrite their development—the field was left to the French-British Concorde consortium and to the Soviets—Congress nevertheless ordered a study of the atmospheric effects of such aircraft.

Two chemists at the University of California at Irvine, F. Sherwood Rowland and Mario Molina, subsequently decided that the chlorofluorocarbons (CFCs) used in refrigerators and aerosol spray cans, and in the manufacture of many insulating plastics, could also affect the ozone layer. They conducted laboratory experiments to demonstrate that sunlight could break the CFCs apart in the stratosphere, releasing chlorine atoms. Because chlorine atoms are extremely reactive, one such atom could destroy millions of ozone atoms. Although it took the CFCs released by spray cans ten to fifteen years to reach the stratosphere, Rowland and Molina estimated that those already released, together with those released in future years, could destroy as much as 30 percent of the ozone level by the middle of the twenty-first century. When the two scientists announced this prediction, it was widely met with howls of laughter; as the chief spokesman, Rowland took the brunt of the ridicule. Cartoonists and stand-up comics had a field day. While people could accept the idea that supersonic planes might be a problem— after all, there were those very visible contrails in the sky from ordinary jets—the idea that spray cans could be agents of doomsday was regarded as hilarious.

It took the public and many politicians a while to grasp the idea that the ozone layer did in fact protect us from catastrophe. As detailed in *The Almanac of Science and Technology*, edited by Richard Golob and Eric Brus, stratospheric ozone, even though it exists only in very small quantities of about three parts per million, serves to screen out 99 percent of the ultraviolet rays that would otherwise bombard the surface of the earth: "Because UV (ultraviolet) radiation can damage nearly all forms of life, most scientists agree that life on earth did not evolve until after the protective ozone layer had formed." Subsequent studies have shown that depletion of the ozone layer could vastly increase skin cancers and cataracts, as well as having possibly severe effects on agricultural yield and ocean plankton, an integral part of the marine food chain.

Within four years of Rowland and Molina's prediction, enough pressure had been brought to bear by scientists and environmental groups to lead Congress to ban the use of CFCs in spray cans. But that was just the start of a much larger and much noisier battle. Because CFCs had so many other uses, from the manufacture of fast-food containers to the cleaning of electronic equipment, industry mounted a major campaign against further curtailment of their use. *The Almanac of Science and Technology* has reported that in the late 1980s, "In the U.S. alone, more than 5,000 businesses at 375,000 locations" used CFCs in manufacturing and service industries, "worth more than $28 billion a year." And as industry fought back, it resurrected the spray-can issue, ridiculing F. Sherwood Rowland once again, and charging that Congress had overreacted to "environmental nuts."

The Environmental Protection Agency stuck to its guns, however, predicting in the spring of 1985 that an increase in the use of CFCs by the current rate of 4.5 percent per year would result in the destruction of not 30 percent but 60 percent of the ozone level by the middle of the coming century. And in the autumn of 1985, the environmental forces had something much more concrete to back up their warnings. At Halley Bay, Antarctica, British meteorologist Joseph Farman discovered the ozone hole, and announced that measurements showed it had been appearing each year since 1976. This led to a seventeen-month study by NASA, which included the participation of hundreds of scientists around the world, as well as two expeditions to Antarctica. Rowland, now justified in his prediction, served on the NASA panel overseeing the research, and Molina, who had gone on to work at NASA's Jet Propulsion Laboratory, provided the scientific explanation as to how CFCs specifically affected the ozone level. In September 1987, forty-six nations put their signature to the Montreal Protocol, agreeing to limit production of CFCs. Industry has since found various alternatives for many uses of CFCs and continues to work to modify its chemical constituents to make it less harmful.

1975 "I don't need bodyguards."

James Hoffa

The *Playboy* interview for June 1975 featured the corrupt former Teamsters' Union boss Jimmy Hoffa. Fresh out of prison, he was trying to regain his power base. Interviewed by Jerry Stanecki, Hoffa played down the degree of animosity his very name aroused in many quarters, and made light of anonymous threats that had been made against him. "I don't need bodyguards," he said succinctly. But on July 30, 1975, Hoffa disappeared, and has never been seen or heard from since. There were those who thought he might just be in hiding, but speculation soon turned to the question of where his body might have been buried. The most colorful answer—and one that some people have always taken seriously—was that he was encased in cement in the foundations of Giants' Stadium, which was being built at the time in New Jersey's Meadowlands.

Hoffa's dismissal of any need for protection is a splendid example of that special category of prediction that is filed under "famous last words."

1977 No need for personal computers in home

Ken Olsen

At a convention of The World Future Society in 1977, Ken Olsen, the founder of Digital Equipment Corporation, said, "There is no reason for any individual to have a computer in his home." Olsen had been the first to offer a major challenge to IBM by making small (by the standards of that time) computers that cost as little as $120,000, instead of the millions needed to invest in an IBM mainframe. In *The Road Ahead*, Bill Gates refers to Olsen as "a legendary hardware designer and a hero of mine, a distant god," and notes that Digital Equipment Corporation "grew to a $6.7 billion company in eight years by offering a wide range of computers in different sizes."

But Olsen simply could not see the commercial possibilities of the personal computer. This failure is often yoked with the infamous statement by IBM head Thomas J. Watson that there was a worldwide market for only about five computers (see 1948). But Watson had been making his judgment on the basis of the huge, vacuum-tube-powered UNIVAC computer then available, and subsequently built the company into the world leader in computers, beginning in the mid-1950s. Ironically, IBM was also slow to grasp the market for personal computers. But Olsen's mistake seems almost inexplicable, since he had pioneered the idea of smaller computers to begin with. By 1982, more than two million personal computers had been sold, and Digital Equipment Corporation finally entered this lucrative market. But it had already lost a crucial edge, and found itself trying to play catch-up.

Computer companies are often accused of getting ahead of themselves, of having visions of future applications that involve excess hype, but the computer business is also littered with the remains of companies that failed to think boldly enough about the future. One decade's foremost genius can all too easily turn into the goat of the next decade. Bill Gates, for example, also recounts the history of An Wang, who switched his company from calculators to word processors at just the right moment and then failed to grasp "the importance of compatible software applications." Gates goes so far as to say that if Wang had foreseen that change, Gates' own company, Microsoft, might not even exist and that he himself might be "a mathematician or an attorney somewhere. . . ."

Just as great scientists like Albert Michelson and Max Born could proclaim "an end to physics" (see 1903) even as revolutionary new discoveries were about to occur, so the geniuses in any field can suddenly lose their perspective, developing a blind spot that leads to notably off-base predictions.

1977 ▶ Concept of parallel worlds

Jack Williamson

Jack Williamson had one of the wildest imaginations of post–World War II science-fiction writers, to the degree that the more conservative writers in the field, and fans who liked their science fiction heavily tilted toward the factual, regarded him as "too much." In fact, Williamson had a very good scientific background; it was just that, given a whiff of a possibility, he would take it further than almost anyone else around. In 1977, Williamson published a novel called *The Legion of Time*. As the distinguished science writer John Gribbin commented in a long note at the end of his book on quantum physics, *In Search of Schrödinger's Cat*, "As far as I have been able to trace, this was the first time, in fact or fiction, that the concept of parallel worlds, later to become the many-worlds interpretation of quantum mechanics, appeared in print."

Many stories and novels had previously been set in alternative present worlds in which everything was different because, for example, the South had won the Civil War or the Nazis had successfully defeated England in the Battle of Britain. But Williamson instead explored the possibility of many alternate realities that existed simultaneously. He wrote his novel only ten years after the basic tenets of quantum mechanics had been set down, and he did so in language that showed he was completely familiar with the field: "Geodesics have an infinite proliferation of possible branches, at the whim of subatomic indeterminism." This may sound like gibberish to the reader unacquainted with quantum mechanics, but as

John Gribbin points out, "Hugh Everett, in his doctoral thesis nineteen years later, couldn't put it any more succinctly, though he did put it on a secure mathematical footing."

What Hugh Everett was dealing with in this famous thesis was the implication of quantum physics that anything that happens in the seemingly solid ("real" if you must) Newtonian world in which we live causes the creation of another complete world in which that event did not take place. These worlds are infinite in number and not actually parallel—instead they branch off one another like endless forks in the road. This theory, which Everett was the first to work out on a sound mathematical basis, may sound crazy, yet it has been shown in many experiments that subatomic particles behave in such bizarre ways that the many-worlds hypothesis is an inevitable mathematical extension of their behavior. It should be said that the many-worlds hypothesis remains deeply controversial; quantum physicists are split down the middle on the subject, with half saying it must be true while the other half says there must be another answer. Indeed, quantum physics is so weird that many people who apply its principles on a daily basis in laser and biological technology, getting real and usable results from employing those principles, still would rather not think much about the theory they are applying.

Whether the many-worlds hypothesis is correct or not—and there are those who would say that it cannot be either proved or disproved from our vantage point, stuck as we are in a world created by our every choice—Jack Williamson was the first to posit the idea in a concrete way. For that reason, John Gribbin concluded his note by saying, "It's seldom that SF really does anticipate the advance of theoretical science, and well worth noting when it does happen."

1979 Nuclear power plants safer than cigarettes

George F. Will

On Friday, March 16, 1979, a new Hollywood technological thriller, starring Jack Lemmon, Jane Fonda, and Michael Douglas, opened in theaters across the country. It was called *The China Syndrome*, a phrase that had been coined in 1965 to describe, in the most alarming terms possible, what would happen if a nuclear accident caused the meltdown of a nuclear reactor, implying that the radioactive fuel would burn a hole from the United States all the way through the earth to China. This was of course a gross exaggeration, as most people understood, but it caught on with the public and made a splendidly apocalyptic movie title.

The *Newsweek* columnist George F. Will was not only a supporter of nuclear power plants but also, like all conservative supporters of the Vietnam War, had never forgiven Jane Fonda for her opposition to the war and her infamous trip to Hanoi in the late 1960s. He could not resist writing a column attacking Fonda's new movie, raking up her past transgressions against "patriotism," and charging her with renewed recklessness on a public issue. In fact, Fonda had only become aroused about nuclear safety in the course of making the movie. It was Jack Lemmon who had the real history of opposition to nuclear power; back in 1971 he had narrated a documentary seen in California in which he said, "nuclear power is not only dirty and undependable . . . it's about as safe as a closet full of cobras." But it was Fonda whom Will chiefly attacked, and in doing so he claimed that nuclear power was safer than sitting next to someone smoking a cigarette on an airplane.

Will was making a flat statement, not a prediction, but in an instance of spectacularly bad timing, he was turned into a false prophet two days after his column appeared. On March 28, there was a serious nuclear accident at the power plant in eastern Pennsylvania known as Three Mile Island. The core did not melt, but the accident ruined the plant and caused near-panic not only in the area around Three Mile Island but deeply alarmed those living anywhere near a nuclear facility, whether in operation or under construction across the country. *The China Syndrome* had had a solid opening week at the box office, but now went on to become a major hit and to garner an Academy Award nomination as Best Picture. George Will was left with the ingredients of an entire omelet on his face, and Sam Donaldson occasionally teased him with sly references to that column for years as they sparred on *This Week with David Brinkley.*

Understandably, Mr. Will never included this commentary in any of his books of collected essays, but to his credit, he continues to support nuclear power to this day, pointing out that the safety features at Three Mile Island did prevent a meltdown, and that the accident at Chernobyl in the Soviet Union in 1986 was due to bad design and upkeep. There are many experts who agree with Mr. Will, and who will point out that the burning of coal and oil have long-term environmental dangers, and that the most deaths from a power accident occurred with the collapse of a hydroelectric dam in Italy in 1963, where 2,500 people were killed outright by the resulting floods. But no new construction has begun on a nuclear power plant in the United States since 1979, and of those that were then being built, several were never completed. The

American public has caught up with George Will's anti-smoking stance, but thanks to Three Mile Island and the impact of *The China Syndrome*, it refused to join him in his enthusiasm for nuclear power.

1980 Asteroid impact as cause of dinosaur extinction

Walter Alvarez and Luis W. Alvarez

In 1973, Walter Alvarez, a geologist from the University of California at Berkeley, was making excavations with a group of colleagues near Gubbio in northern Italy. They were searching for evidence marking the reversals of the Earth's magnetic field which take place every ten thousand years on average, for unknown reasons. At Gubbio, he found a clear demarcation in the limestone, where a layer of clay almost devoid of fossils was sandwiched between two layers of limestone filled with fossils. The clay appeared at a point that coincided with the end of the Cretaceous period, when dinosaurs disappeared from the Earth 65 million years ago. Four years later, he brought some samples of this clay back to the United States and discussed what he had found with his father, the Nobel Prize–winning physicist Luis M. Alvarez.

Although he was essentially a particle physicist, Luis Alvarez had an exceptionally broad range of scientific interests. Intrigued by the Gubbio clay, he began testing its geochemical makeup. Working with additional samples collected in 1978, Luis Alvarez found that there was a concentration of iridium in the clay that was thirty times as concentrated as in the limestone either above or below. Iridium is a rare element on the Earth's surface, but is common in meteorites. That there should be a much larger amount of iridium in the clay from the time of the mass extinction of the dinosaurs was an astonishing discovery. What could have caused such a large amount of iridium to have settled on the Earth at that time? The possibility of detritus from a nearby supernova was considered; if a star had exploded in the near reaches of our galaxy, it could have subsequently deposited iridium on the Earth. But this hypothesis was not sufficiently supported by other evidence, and Luis and Walter turned to another idea: that a meteorite at least ten kilometers in diameter had impacted on our planet. Such a massive body would have caused vast dust clouds to blanket the planet for as long as several years, shutting out sunlight and destroying plant life from algae to forests, bringing on a disastrous collapse of the food chain. That would explain the mass extinction of so many species evident in the fossil record of that period. That mass extinction not only wiped out the dinosaurs, it left vast numbers of evolutionary niches to be filled, giving rise to the great diversification of mammalian life that eventually led to the evolution of human beings.

These were exciting ideas, simple enough to be easily conveyed in the popular press, and the Alvarezes' theory was given wide coverage after their now famous report was published in the journal *Science* in June 1980. Since this was a revolutionary theory, scientific reaction ranged from enthusiastic to extremely skeptical. But it was a testable theory. How common was the presence of iridium in the geological record not just at Gubbio but in other locales around the earth? Could the crater left by such an asteroid impact be found, perhaps beneath the sea?

The presence of iridium in similar concentrations, laid down at the same time, was confirmed at locations around the globe within the next two years. But the crater remained a problem. And other scientists began raising new questions. One study cast grave doubts on how long the iridium particles could have remained in the stratosphere, allowing them to be distributed by wind currents. But that led to a new and more plausible explanation for the creation of a long-term dust cloud—ballistic dispersal, which computer models showed to be feasible. Even so, many biologists and geologists clung to older theories holding that the extinction of the dinosaurs and other animals had taken place much more gradually.

The Alvarez theory got an enormous boost at the end of 1993, however, when measurements were concluded on a huge crater that had been found several years earlier at the bottom of the Gulf of Mexico. The measurements showed that the crater was much larger than initially thought, with a diameter of 186 miles. This was not only larger than the state of West Virginia, it made it the largest known crater on any planet in the solar system. Initial tests showed the crater to have been formed 65 million years ago, exactly in accord with the Alvarez theory. Over the next few years, exhaustive tests were carried out on material brought up from the bottom of the crater. In early 1997, scientists were able to say that the iridium and other deposits were consistent with the findings already established in surface rocks around the world. There was no longer any question that this was the result of the asteroid impact that Walter and Luis Alvarez had claimed must have occurred.

1984 Cyberspace
(Virtual Reality)

William Gibson

William Gibson was one of the leading figures in the development of new directions for science fiction writing in the 1980s. Some older writers (and fans) hated this new approach, objecting to its "punk sensibility," its "anarchic" ideas and its jazzy, "hyperbolic" style. But the men and women writing this fresh, vivid fiction became extremely popular, anyway, none more so than William Gibson. It was only fitting that Gibson should invent the word "cyberspace" in his 1984 novel *Neuromancer*: "Cyberspace. A consensual hallucination experienced daily by billions of legitimate operators, in every nation, by children being taught mathematical concepts . . . A graphic representation of data abstracted from the banks of every computer in the human system. Unthinkable complexity. Lines of light ranged in the non-space of the mind, clusters and constellations of data. Like city lights, receding."

The word "cyberspace" was quickly co-opted by the mass media as a useful term for the new universes of knowledge and communications created by computer technology in general and the Internet in particular. But Gibson had something more specific and more unsettling in mind—the future world of virtual reality. He envisioned a world in which the more daring individuals would use sensors to connect their own nervous systems directly to the global computer system he called "the Matrix." He called this kind of connection between flesh and electronic "jacking in," a term that elicited the obviously expected nervousness in some quarters.

Howard Rheingold's 1991 book *Virtual Reality* remains the best over-all guide to this new world and how it came about, although there have been many technical developments since he wrote it. "Imagine a wraparound television with three-dimensional programs," he wrote, "including three-dimension sound, and solid objects that you can pick up and manipulate, even feel with your fingers and hands. . . . Imagine that you are the creator as well as the consumer of your artificial experience, with a power to use a gesture or word to remold the world you see and hear and feel. That part is not fiction." Using head-mounted displays (HMDs) and Argonne remote manipulators (ARMs), together with three-dimensional computer graphics, Rheingold had already experienced many virtual environments when he wrote his book. Virtual reality had already become a tool in many fields from surgery to architecture, allowing physicians to rehearse operations and architects to "walk through" buildings they were designing.

But although virtual reality holds the promise of innumerable applications that will greatly aid humanity, from cancer research to providing new ways for the disabled to interact with the world, the media has tended to sensationalize it from the start. Rheingold notes that the media quickly jumped on a comment by the late Jerry Garcia of the Grateful Dead, who said, "They made LSD illegal. I wonder what they're going to do about this stuff." Rheingold's publishers naturally took advantage of the quote as well, putting it on the back jacket along with Arthur C. Clarke's prediction that virtual reality "won't merely replace TV. It will eat it alive." The "head trip" aspects of virtual reality bother a number of experts, but the possibility that really upsets the alarmists is virtual sex. The idea of putting on a helmet, conjuring up an image of anyone you choose on a video screen, and then having sex with that image with all the sensory experiences that are the fruit of actual sex, sends the self-appointed guardians of sexual morality into an absolute tizzy. But experts in the field think that is still quite a long way off, still very much in the imaginations of science fiction writers like William Gibson. On the other hand, Gibson gave us the word "cyberspace"; maybe we need to take at least some of his visions quite seriously.

1987 ▶ The end of universities

Herbert I. London

The May–June 1987 issue of the serious trend-spotting journal *The Futurist* carried a pessimistic article by Herbert I. London. Then dean of the Gallatin Division of New York University, London was not happy to write the words, "I am convinced the university as an institution cannot survive." But London was also a senior fellow of the renowned "think tank," the Hudson Institute, which has specialized in bringing the views of disparate experts to bear on many high-profile issues. In his article for *The Futurist*, London focused on a number of problems facing American universities. The combination of escalating costs for higher education and a dwindling number of students as the baby boom ended was creating a crunch to which the only answer seemed to be even higher tuition costs for students. In addition, he noted a growing public disenchantment with higher education because of its elitist reputation, never helpful in a country with a historical strain of anti-intellectualism. The fall-off in federal funds for research, partially because of economic downsizing but also because of public discomfort with university involvement in military research, was also cited.

Since 1987, all of the problems London touched on have intensified. Costs at the country's top private universities are approaching $30,000 per year for undergraduates; even public institutions are considering various steps that would make it more difficult to attend college. Many in academia itself feel that the still-growing trend toward political correctness is undercutting standards, which in turn can only devalue the value of higher education. Every spring, the news media are full of stories about how difficult it is for that year's graduates in the arts and humanities to find jobs that make use of their particular skills and knowledge. As research funding continues to erode, it becomes more difficult for all but the most famous institutions to attract teachers of the highest quality. And with increasing specialization, technical and business colleges often seem a better value than a liberal arts education. Thus, the problems that London took note of a decade ago have only become more intense.

But does that really mean that the university in its present form can't survive, as London concluded? Some educators contend that exactly because the broad-based liberal arts education is losing its appeal, it becomes more important than ever to preserve it as a bastion against a dumbed-down, relentlessly present-tense society. Yet most proposed solutions to the problem envision a financial security for universities based on a great increase in outreach courses channeled to students over computer linkups—and this in itself is at odds with one of the primary functions of a liberal arts education—the shared learning experience of students from diverse backgrounds brought together in a single place. Graduates of even the most famous universities, like Yale, M.I.T. and Stanford, will often say that the most valuable asset they took away from such institutions was the stimulus and friendship of other students. In an increasingly technological society, that very human element of the university experience may prove to be the most important of all, and serve as a rationale for the survival of at least some universities in a form not all that different from their twentieth-century form. Higher education as such may well be obtainable in many other ways in the twenty-first century, but if the atmosphere and kinds of human interaction that have long marked university life become more difficult to obtain, that in itself may become the reason for their continued existence. In this context, it is worth noting that the best attended conventions of the late twentieth century are those for people who work in the field of computers.

1994 ▸ Comet Shoemaker-Levy 9 will disappoint

Nature

In an essay collected in his book *Dinosaur in a Haystack*, Stephen Jay Gould takes note of a 1994 headline in the British magazine *Nature*: "Comet Shoemaker-Levy 9—the big fizzle is coming." This comet had been discovered in March of 1993 by Gene and Carolina Shoemaker, together with David Levy. It was the ninth such body this team of comet-watchers had been the first to see, and it would prove to be their most important discovery. What made it remarkable was that it had a decaying orbit that would cause it to smash into the atmosphere of the planet Jupiter in July 1994. With luck, this impact would produce a display on the upper surface of Jupiter's enormously thick atmosphere that would reveal many things about both Jupiter itself and the behavior of comets. Teams of astronomers around the world were thus set to monitor the impact. Hopes for a great display were tempered by the fact that the comet would hit Jupiter's atmosphere on its night side, hidden from our view, but because of the planet's rapid rotation, the area of impact would spin into focus only a few minutes later. Nevertheless, the fact that moment of collision would be hidden, taken together with the fact that the recent appearance of Halley's Comet, making its usual seventy-six-year visit, and the approach of the newly discovered comet called Kohoutek, had both been very disappointing in terms of visual display, *Nature* had decided to lower expectations ahead of time.

This advance downgrading of the event proved to be a great mistake. The scars left by the impact of all twenty-one fragments of the comet (it had already broken apart when first seen) were brilliantly visible, some of them causing disruptions in the Jovian atmosphere as large as the Earth itself. Since Stephen Jay Gould writes for the American journal *Natural History*, it no doubt gave him a chuckle to report on the mistake made by its British rival. But of course the shoe could well have been on the other foot. No one knew what the result would be, and scientists were in fact astonished and thrilled that this collision between comet and planet turned out to be the event of the century in our solar system. The reappearance of Halley's Comet in 1986 had been hyped to the skies and turned out to be very disappointing. It was perfectly sensible to err on the side of caution this time around. But that's exactly what makes the art of prediction so precarious—being perfectly sensible can get you in as much trouble as reckless optimism.

1995 The Internet as a self-publishing medium

Bill Gates

In *The Road Ahead*, Bill Gates writes, "To get a book into print a publisher has to agree to pay the up-front expense of manufacturing, distribution, and marketing. The information highway will create a medium with entry barriers lower than any we have ever seen. The Internet is the greatest self-publishing vehicle ever. Its bulletin boards have demonstrated some of the changes that will occur when everyone has access to low-friction distribution and individuals can post messages, images, or software of their own creation."

This sounds wonderful. But there are those who have serious doubts about this vision of a wonderfully creative future for everyone. Clifford Stoll, a University of California professor with a creative background in computer technology, brings up some pertinent problems in his book *Silicon Snake Oil*. He notes that the Internet has no editors, unlike publishers; no reviewers, which do exist for books; and no Dewey decimal system, which makes it possible for us to easily locate books in a library. Even Bill Gates recognizes that there is "a lot of garbage on the Internet," but Stoll emphasizes that one of the things that editors at book companies do is to screen out an enormous amount of that garbage in the first place. Moreover, if the ideas in a book manuscript are good enough, a book publisher will put the creator of those ideas together with an experienced writer, ghostwriter, or editor to whip the material into publishable shape. There's no question that book editors have their own blind spots, and there are books that get turned down by all the major publishers and go on to become great popular successes. Bill Gates mentions a good example, the novel *The Bridges of Madison County*. The fact that most book reviewers hated that novel may say something about both reviewers and the taste of the reading public, but the animosity of critics certainly didn't stop it from becoming an extraordinary best-seller. The fact that book reviewers also have their blind spots doesn't mean they aren't a valuable part of the publishing system. Their enthusiasm leads readers to far more books that might otherwise go unnoticed than their bad reviews turn off readers of books that are going to be popular anyway. Without reviewers, what gets published on the Internet has to be sorted through by the individual on his own time, and it can take plenty of it.

The lack of an equivalent to the Dewey decimal system on the Internet is a different matter. While it is true that experienced Internet users can eventually find what they're looking for, Stoll and other critics insist that it takes more expertise and time than Internet enthusiasts are willing to admit. This point of contention may eventually be answered by software developments that are still just blips on the horizon. But such a development, according to many experts, including both Internet boosters and doubters, is likely to have to await a formalized method for paying royalties to those who self-publish on the Internet. Bill Gates is sure this can be managed down the line, but as things stand there are still vast legal tangles to be resolved concerning payment to original authors whose work is published by major companies, let alone compensation for self-publishing.

Aside from the question of quality and easy access, there is another underlying problem that could affect the future of self-publishing on the Internet. Stoll takes note of it in regard to on-line interviews: "Since readers often skip arguments that take up more than a screenful, electronic meetings simplify complex issues. This encourages short, simple questions, and equally concise replies. Just as television gives us soundbites, the on-line interview provides one-line answers." This suggests that Internet self-publishing may have a less expansive future than Gates and his fellow optimists suggest.

1995 ▶ The wallet PC

Bill Gates

In 1863, Jules Verne predicted the fax machine in his novel *Paris in the Twentieth Century*, which was rejected by his publisher on the grounds that its world of the 1960s would be unbelievable to his readers. In fact, it took a little more than a hundred years for the fax machine to become commonplace. Writing in 1995, Bill Gates devoted several pages in his book *The Road Ahead* to the concept of a multi-use personal computer the size of a conventional wallet. This idea has been around for a while, but Gates places particular emphasis on it, and expects it to become reality not in another century but in the near future—he confidently addresses the uses to which the reader of his book will be putting such a miniaturized computer.

"It will display messages and schedules and also let you read or send electronic mail and faxes, monitor weather and stock reports, and play both simple and sophisticated games. At a meeting you might take notes, check your appointments, browse information if you're bored, or choose from among thousands of easy-to-call-up photos of your kids." He goes on to say that "Tomorrow the wallet PC will make it easy for anyone to spend and accept digital funds. Your wallet will link you into a store's computer to allow money to be transferred without any physical exchange at a cash register. Digital cash will be used in interpersonal transactions, too. If your son needs money, you might digitally slip five bucks from your wallet PC to his."

Reading about this wondrous little computer can make a reader slightly giddy. How about having Dick Tracy's wristwatch telephone, imagined by Charles Gould in the 1930s, to go with it? They could be sold in sets. But Gates is quite serious, and in purely technological terms there is ample evidence that both these devices are feasible in the near future. Back in 1964, Gordon E. Moore, who was then at the Fairchild company but went on to become a cofounder of Intel, pointed out that the number of circuits on a given chip was doubling every year, and the price coming down in direct proportion. He predicted that that would continue. It did for ten years, and he then predicted that the doubling would take place every two years. Moore's Law, as it has come to be called, makes the wallet PC eminently possible in technical terms.

But just because something can be done does not necessarily mean that the public will want it (see 1968 for the case of the visual telephone). One of the main challenges to be met in terms of the wallet PC involves security. Gates addresses these issues squarely, but since he wrote his book more and more concerns have been expressed about computer security problems; an entirely new class of criminals has arisen to take advantage of computer technology. There is also a privacy issue: will people want to have so much of their lives encoded in a wallet-sized machine that can all too easily be lost or stolen?

Unlike Jules Verne's "unbelievable" fax machine, Gates's wallet PC is fundamentally credible right now. But that doesn't necessarily mean that people will want it. Gates believes that a top-of-the-line model will initially cost about $1,000. As has been shown in respect to many new technologies, the VCR being a prime example, a kind of commercial synergy must be established in which enough people are willing to pay top price for something before its full potential is realized, which in turn brings down the price to the point where everyone wants it. Sometimes that happens, sometimes it does not. The wallet PC will be a major test of how much computer technology people ultimately want.

1996 Solar power primary in 21st Century

Senator Edward M. Kennedy

In 1996, Daniel M. Berman and John T. O'Connor published a book called *Who Owns the Sun?*, with a dust jacket embellished by quotes from several eminent people. Senator Edward M. Kennedy said, "Solar energy may well become the primary energy source for America and the world in the twenty-first century." Senator Kennedy has, of course, long been counted an important friend to environmental activists, for whom solar power is a major interest. Note, however, the politician's slight hedge in the use of the words "may well." Another jacket quote came from one of the most aggressive environmentalists, Barry Commoner, whose tone is typically apocalyptic: "If human society is to survive, the transition to a solar-based economy is inevitable."

The book itself issues a stirring call for the use of solar power, but it also traces the history of this energy source in a way that suggests Kennedy's slight hint of caution is the wiser course. The use of the sun's power to heat water, as shown by archeological digs in the Middle East, goes back to before the birth of Christ, in the form of roof tanks painted black to trap the sun's energy. In more modern times, the first solar water heater of any sophistication was invented by Clarence E. Kemp of Baltimore in 1891. A few decades later, a heater called "Day & Night," invented by William J. Bailey, sold a thousand units in California in 1920, after being on the market for several years. With the advent of solar panels that could be used to provide electricity for an entire building, solar power made real progress in the 1970s. This did not sit well with the big gas, oil, and electric power companies, and in 1984 both Ronald Reagan, on the national level, and the Republican gubernatorial candidate in California, George Deukmejian, made campaign promises to end income-tax credits for energy-renewable projects like solar and wind power. Solar power was a $415-million industry in 1984; without the tax credits, it plummeted to a $20-million industry in 1986.

Solar energy has fared better in some foreign countries, like Japan, which must import all its fossil fuels, and India, where rural areas are often without power plants or distribution systems. Tokyo alone had a million and a half solar water heaters in use in 1991. Even in the

United States, the picture is brightening again, especially in western states where environmental consciousness is high. According to a March 1997 report in *The New York Times*, a survey by a major utility company in the Southwest found that its customers were willing to pay from $5 to $7 more per month to support the use of solar power. The political tide also seems to have turned again. As the *Times* reports, "With its [energy] deregulation law, California is dedicating a little less than 1 percent of every electric bill to supporting research as well as programs for green power; the fund is expected to total about $540 million by 2002." Alternative energy research has also been supported by the Clinton administration, but it remains to be seen whether Congress will go along with the requested increase in funds.

In the coming years, another oil crisis could once again increase interest in solar power, and other alternatives like wind power. But a tug of war between the entrenched fossil fuel forces and green power advocates seems likely to continue to cause many ups and downs for solar power unless costs can be brought down to the level of fossil fuels or below. It now seems that that may be possible in the near future if advances in semiconductor technology continue to enhance the efficiency of the photovoltaic cells that are used to convert sunlight to electricity. As always, it is when new technology become more cost-efficient than old technology that sweeping changes take place. If that happens with solar energy, then the predictions of Senator Kennedy and Barry Commoner may indeed prove correct.

1996 ▶ Privacy to be major 21st Century concern

Marc Rotenberg

In a September 1996 article in *The New York Times Magazine* by James Gleick, Marc Rotenberg, the director of the Electronic Privacy Information Center of Washington, D.C., is quoted as saying, "Privacy will be to the information economy of the next century what consumer protection and environmental concerns have been to the industrial society of the twentieth century." Gleick's article begins by pointing out that the kind of "Big Brother" surveillance predicted by George Orwell in his 1948 novel *1984* did not come to pass. What he does not point out is that it was in 1984 that another novelist, William Gibson, coined the word "cyberspace," which has found an important place in our language as a term to describe the ever more pervasive electronic world that surrounds us.

That electronic world has been ballyhooed as promising a world of increased knowledge and interconnectedness by means of an "Information Highway" that will be accessible to most people on the planet. But no such technological revolution comes without costs, and many experts are increasingly worried about what the nature of those costs may be. Those worries include economic displacement through the loss of existing jobs, the reduction of knowledge to oversimplified computer bytes instead of sound bites, the rampant proliferation of rumor instead of fact, and a further erosion of cultural standards. But questions about privacy have become particularly intense. Even in the six months since Gleick's article appeared there have been several stories that have gotten major news coverage. The arrest of a university graduate student for the seduction of a young woman over the Internet, followed by her alleged rape, tied into numerous stories about the amount of pornography on the Internet, and the ease with which child-molesters can access information about children, including names and addresses. On a more general level, a Web site posted by the Social Security Administration in order to make it easier for taxpayers to get information about their own government financial records was quickly withdrawn when questions were raised about the security of such information. Thousands of requests for information from this Web site had been denied because incorrect access information had been supplied—did this mean that the security system was working well or that a great many people were trying to get hold of information to which they had no right about other people's lives? The degree to which every aspect of our lives is being electronically encoded, from financial and medical records to our consumer habits, right down to the groceries we purchase, was suddenly starting to worry the average citizen instead of just the experts. Governments and large corporations have expensive programs to develop codes designed to protect privileged information—but what about the rest of us? Even at government and corporate levels, serious questions remain as to whether any access code can be devised that a determined computer hacker cannot break through. As the average citizen becomes more aware of such high-level concerns, he or she feels increasingly vulnerable.

Thus Marc Rotenberg's prediction that electronic privacy will become a major issue in the coming century seems to be right on the mark. The question that remains unanswered is whether it will be possible to create adequate protections—and what will happen to the Information Highway if those protections prove inadequate.

1996 Pinpoint weather forecasting

National Weather Service

In late 1996, the National Weather Service claimed that within five to ten years, it would be possible to forecast the weather so far in advance, and so accurately, that people would be able to choose a vacation spot weeks in advance and arrive to find just the kind of weather they expected and wanted. Never mind that three months later, the same organization was saying that cutbacks in funding had made it more difficult to keep track of even dangerous storms, like hurricanes, that could cause heavy damage. Even if the funding is available to invest in the computer technology essential to future pinpoint weather forecasting, a question remains as to whether such accuracy is possible at all.

It is true that weather forecasting has improved considerably in the last two decades, largely as a result of Doppler radar systems. Previous instruments could measure the location and intensity of precipitation, but Doppler instruments can also measure the speed with which precipitation is moving toward or away from the radar. These instruments have made it possible to predict more accurately when a weather system will move into a given region. Doppler radar has even improved the ability to warn of tornado formations, which coalesce and dissipate with great rapidity. But forecasters are still unable to give adequate warning of nearly 30 percent of the tornadoes that occur. These storms, however, are the most difficult problem in weather forecasting, and because they are local and sporadic, a lack of complete success in pinpointing them doesn't by itself invalidate the overall idea of being able to predict regional weather weeks in advance.

The combination of Doppler radar, increasingly detailed satellite observations, improved analytical computer programs, and developments in many other more restricted areas of weather observation, should, in terms of usual logic, portend ever more accurate forecasting in the future. But there is an underlying problem that has nothing to do with usual logic. That problem goes by the name of chaos theory. Evidence to support this theory was long resisted by scientists—it was often thrown away as a "spoiled" experiment. But quantum physicists, followed by chemists, began to wonder if these supposed examples of experiments run amok were not in fact telling us something fundamental about how the universe works. In the simplest terms, chaos theory suggests that there is an aspect of nature that refuses to obey the usual laws of matter, space, time, and gravity, and that under certain circumstances, this haywire aspect of nature overwhelms everything else in ways that produce unexpected, and wondrous, results. Scientists who have come to specialize in chaos theory in the last twenty years believe that it may explain many puzzles, throughout the sciences, that are puzzles only if one tries to shoehorn them into pigeonholes where they refuse to properly fit. If one accepts chaos—utterly unpredictable results—in certain circumstances, and is willing to view it as a kind of anti-law that is as important as the established laws that govern cause and effect, then many mysteries, including perhaps the big bang that gave birth to the universe, become more understandable.

If chaos theory is valid, then nothing, especially anything as complex as weather patterns, is going to become predictable beyond a certain point. Chaos theory in fact has special application to weather, since one of its crucial elements was first identified in respect to a study of weather forecasting. In 1963, a professor of meteorology at the Massachusetts Institute of Technology, Edward Lorenz, sought to explain why weather forecasts so often proved incorrect. As described in *The Arrow of Time* by Peter Coveny and Roger Highfield, Lorenz used a computer "to make as simple a mathematic model of atmospheric weather flow as possible, while retaining the essential physics." Coming up with "a set of three coupled non-linear differential equations . . . he gradually realized that however slight the variation in the initial weather conditions fed into the computer which solved the equations, the resulting solutions (the weather forecast) changed totally in a very short time."

What Lorenz had stumbled on was a factor that would not even be named for another ten years—a "strange attractor," the anomaly that sparks the creation of chaotic patterns. Lorenz used an extremely captivating image to convey what he had found—he said that the beating of a butterfly's wings in the Amazon basin could introduce a variable that would subsequently create a hurricane in the West Indies. Later, when chaos theory had become a cohesive theoretical discipline, Lorenz's strange attractor was named after him.

If chaos theory is correct—and not only is it mathematically sound, but the conditions to set it in motion can be created in advanced chemical and physics experiments—then no amount of data will ever be enough to make it possible to predict the weather in a given area weeks in advance.

But it's not just weather prediction that is in trouble here. The quantum mechanics from which chaos theory derives have implications for predictions in general. One of the foundations of quantum physics is the indeterminacy principle published by Werner Heisenberg in 1927, work for which he would receive the Nobel Prize in Physics in 1932. Heisenberg showed that in quantum physics it was possible to measure the exact position of a particular subatomic particle at a specific moment, *or* to determine the exact trajectory of that particle. But it wasn't possible to do both. The act of taking one kind of measurement changed the other aspect of the particle's very existence. The cloud chamber used to measure the trajectory will also slow down the progress of a proton, for instance, so that it becomes impossible to know where it is at a specific moment in time. The radiation used to pinpoint its location at a moment in time, on the other hand, will give the proton a tiny shove that will change its trajectory. Timothy Ferris explains this problem superbly in his book *Coming of Age in the Milky Way.* He concludes that Heisenberg demonstrated "that we can *never* know everything about the behavior of even one particle, much less myriads of them, and, therefore, can never make predictions about the future that will be completely accurate in every detail."

As this book has shown, predictions can be made that get things so close to exactly right that we are amazed by the accuracy of the prognostication. But Jules Verne was off by two miles in his astonishing prediction about where a spacecraft that had been to the moon and back would land in the Pacific, and many of his predictions never came true at all. There is no inland canal from the sea to the center of Paris. Einstein was correct about matter warping space, and the measurements taken in 1919 during an eclipse of the sun almost exactly matched his predictions. Almost. Enough to prove him correct, but still not precisely on the money. Thus, if another book like this one is published a hundred years from now, whether in printed form or broadcast by electronic means on whatever the Internet has become, it will mostly likely contain references to predictions about the future being made right now, at the conclusion of the twentieth century, some of them remarkably prescient—getting things *almost* right—and some of them laughably wrong. And that's a prediction!

BIBLIOGRAPHY

Aldiss, Brian. *The Trillion Year Spree*. New York: Atheneum, 1986.

Asimov, Issac. *The Relativity of Wrong*. New York: Doubleday, 1988.

Asimov, Issac and Janet. *Frontiers II*. New York: Dutton, Truman Talley Books, 1993.

Baldwin, Neil. *Edison: Inventing the Century*. New York: Hyperion, 1995.

Breuer, William B. *Race to the Moon*. Wesport, CN: Praeger, 1992.

Bronowski, Jacob. *The Ascent of Man*. Boston: Little, Brown, 1973.

Cerf, Christopher, and Victor Navasky. *The Experts Speak*. New York: Bantam, 1984.

Cheney, Margaret. *Tesla: Man Out of Time*. Englewood Cliffs, NJ: Prentice Hall, 1981.

Clark, Wilson. *Energy for Survival*. New York: Doubleday Anchor, 1974.

Clarke, Arthur C. *2001: A Space Odyssey*. New York: Ballentine, 1968.

Clymer, Flody. *Those Wonderful Old Automobiles*. Bethesda, MD: Bonanza, 1953.

Commoner, Barry. *The Closing Circle*. New York: Knopf, 1971.

Cornish, Edward, ed. *The 1990s and Beyond*. Bethesda, MD: World Future Society, 1990.

Coveny, Peter, and Roger Highfield. *The Arrow of Time*. New York: Ballantine, 1990.

Davie, Michael. *Titanic*. New York: Knopf, 1986.

Dreyfus, Herbert and Stuart. *Mind Over Machine*. New York: Free Press, 1986.

Dubos, Rene. *Man Adapting*. New Haven: Yale University Press, 1965.

Erlich, Paul R. *The Population Bomb*. New York: Ballantine, 1971.

Ferris, Timothy, *Coming of Age in the Milky Way*. New York: Morrow, 1988.

Forrester, Tom. *High Tech Society*. Cambridge, MA: MIT Press, 1987.

Gamow, George. *One, Two, Three . . . Infinity*. New York: Mentor, 1960.

Gates, Bill. *The Road Ahead*. New York: Viking, 1995.

Gibbs-Smith, L. H. *Flight Through the Ages*. New York: Crowell, 1974.

Golob, Richard, and Eric Brus, eds. *The Almanac of Science and Technology*. New York: Harcourt, Brace, Jovanovitch, 1990.

Gould, Stephen Jay. *Dinosaur in a Haystack*. New York: Harmony Books, 1995.

Gribbin, John. *In Search of Schrödinger's Cat*. New York: Bantam, 1984.

Gribbin, John, and Martin Rees. *Cosmic Coincidences*. New York: Bantam, 1989.

Kiplinger's Looking Ahead. Washington, D.C.: Kiplinger Books, 1993.

Latour, Bruno. *Aramis, or the Love of Technology*. Cambridge, MA: Harvard University Press, 1996.

Malone, John. *The World War II Quiz Book*. New York: Morrow, Quill, 1991.

McLuhan, Marshall. *Understanding Media*. New York: McGraw Hill, 1964.

McLuhan, Marshall, and Bruce R. Powers. *The Global Village*. New York: Oxford University Press, 1989.

Miller, Walter James. *The Annotated Jules Verne: From the Earth to the Moon*. New York: Grammercy Books, 1995.

Muller, John. *Astaire Dancing*. New York: Knopf, 1985.

Petroski, Henry. *The Evolution of Useful Things*. New York: Knopf, 1997.

Porter, Ray. *Man Masters Nature*. New York: George Braziller, 1988.

Rheingold, Howard. *Virtual Reality*. New York: Touchstone, 1991.

Roberts, Royston M. *Serendipity*. New York: Wiley, 1989.

Sagan, Carl. *Cosmos*. New York: Random House, 1980.

———. *The Demon Haunted World*. New York: Random House, 1995.

———. *Pale Blue Dot*. New York: Random House, 1993.

Stearn, Jess. *The Sleeping Prophet*. New York: Doubleday, 1967.

Stoll, Clifford. *Silicon Snake Oil*. New York: Anchor, 1996.

Toffler, Alvin. *Future Shock*. New York: Random House, 1970.

———. *Previews and Premises*. New York: Morrow, 1983.

Vacca, Roberto. *The Coming Dark Age*. New York: Doubleday, 1973.

Verne, Jules. *Paris in the Twentieth Century*. New York: Random House, 1996.

Wallichinsky, David. *The 20th Century*. Little Brown, 1995.

Wiener, Norbert. *Cybernetics*. New York: Wiley, 1948.

Wilford, John Noble. *The Riddle of the Dinosaurs*. New York: Knopf, 1986.

Zubin, Robert, with Richard Wagner. *The Case for Mars*. New York: Free Press, 1997.

INDEX OF PREDICTIONS

INDEX OF PREDICTORS